Beyond
the Secret

Beyond the Secret

Spiritual Power and the Law of Attraction

 Dr. Lisa Love

HAMPTON ROADS

This edition first published in 2011 by
Hampton Roads Publishing Company
Charlottesville, VA

ISBN: 978-1-57174-672-6
Library of Congress Cataloging-in-Publication Data is available upon request.

Cover by Jim Warner
Typeset in Adobe Garamond Pro
Typeset by Jane Hagaman

Printed in Canada
TCP
10 9   8 7 6 5 4 3 2 1
The paper used in this publication meets the minimum requirements of the
American National Standard for Information Sciences—Permanence of Paper
for Printed Library Materials Z39.48-1992 (R1997).

This book is joyfully dedicated to all those who seek to bring greater love, light, and spiritual power to the world. May they prosper and succeed mightily in that quest, wherever and whoever they are!

The greatest use of life is to spend it on something that will outlast it.

—William James

Contents

Part I. Spiritual Attraction: Ten Basic Steps

THE ONE STAGE
Getting in Touch with Spirit

THE TWO STAGE
Developing a Mental Understanding

THE THREE STAGE
Manifesting What Spirit Wants

Part II. Living What Spirit Wants:
Practical Applications

Introduction to
the Revised Edition

As of 2011, it's plain to see that something is shifting around the world. In just a few short years, we have experienced a global financial meltdown, oil spills, tsunamis, earthquakes, and uprisings and revolts in many countries. From a law of attraction standpoint, what is going on here? Actually, something very positive, because these events are giving us the opportunity to use the law of attraction to create a whole new world for humankind, one where the law of attraction will be used more along the lines of contribution, spiritual principles, and making a contribution to others, than for material and consumptive purposes.

After all, much of what we have attracted to ourselves in the past fifty years has been dictated by a belief system that has increasingly influenced our political, social, economic, and even religious views stating that our main goal in life is to be consumers.. This belief system was in many ways shaped by leading economist Victor Lebow, who defined the "meaning of life" in 1955 in this way:

> Our enormously productive economy demands that we make consumption our way of life, that we convert the buying and use of goods into rituals, that we seek our spiritual satisfactions, our ego satisfactions, in consumption. The measure of social status, of social acceptance, of prestige, is now to be found in our consumptive patterns. The very meaning and significance of our

lives today [are] expressed in consumptive terms. . . . The greater the pressures upon the individual to conform to safe and accepted social standards, the more does he tend to express his aspirations and his individuality in terms of what he wears, drives, eats, his home, his car, his pattern of food serving, his hobbies.

As if that weren't enough, Lebow goes on to say that when creating a consumptive hunger in people:

These commodities and services must be offered to the consumer with a special urgency. We require not only "forced draft" consumption, but "expensive" consumption as well. We need things consumed, burned up, worn out, replaced, and discarded at an ever increasing pace. We need to have people eat, drink, dress, ride, live, with ever more complicated and, therefore, constantly more expensive consumption.

With such a doctrine leading the way for decades, it's easy to see how we have used the law of attraction to create lifestyles of consumption, including expensive consumption, excessive consumption, have-everything-you-want consumption, and discard items as fast as possible, moving on to wanting more, even if these patterns destroy our world.

Fortunately, in light of current crises, Lebow's notions of consumption as the meaning of life don't feel so good anymore. Thank goodness! I knew they wouldn't. As early as January 2008, right after *Beyond the Secret* came out, I was already predicting in radio interviews that because of our excessive focus on greed and consumption, a worldwide economic collapse and revolt was coming. It did, starting later that very year. In the middle of this shift, we have been given a tremendous opportunity to create a new story—a new meaning of life—in which the law of attraction will no longer be based upon principles of consumption, but upon spiritual principles that allow for the discovery of how each of us can make a contribution to the world as we become more conscious, connected, creative, compassionate, concerned, and caring individuals.

The end result? More joy, less happiness. Though it might seem like a picky parsing of words, for me, happiness is an arbitrary emotion belonging to the level of the ego. That's because we tend to feel happy when things go our way, and unhappy when they do not. But joy is different. Joy exists even if we are not particularly happy on a personal level. That may be why there is no such word in the English language as "unjoyful." Joy comes about when we feel good by doing good. Like a really nutritious meal, joy doesn't give us just a quick happiness fix; it sustains us for a much longer period. Joy arises when we know we can sleep well at night because we did our best to make a positive difference in the lives of those we care about. So, yes, the world is going through turbulence and change. But while that may make us unhappy now, it could make us that much more joyful in the future!

With joy we will also use the law of attraction to create a world that benefits everyone, not just ourselves. That is why I am not only joyful, I have a tremendous feeling of optimism and hope. Care to be more joyful, too? Then I know the ideas in this book, which teach how to use the law of attraction in a more spiritual way, will help you.

Preface

The Secret

In 2006, millions of people discovered the book, *The Secret* by Rhonda Byrne, in which they learned about the law of attraction and its ability to help you get whatever you want in life. The book was a huge success, and rightfully so. Dozens of illumed minds came together and contributed their talents and wisdom to help free their fellow human beings of the restrictive thinking patterns keeping them from living the lives of their dreams. What a noble and beneficial cause!

Yet, *The Secret* is not without controversy. Many stellar and bright people have called its assertions into question. Some people in the psychological field worry that *The Secret* will cause individuals to blame themselves in an unhealthy way for every difficult situation they encounter in their lives—even rape, torture, and genocide. Numerous physicians fear that *The Secret's* statements regarding health (such as that all illness is caused by people not thinking and feeling in a positive way) seriously trivialize the multiple factors that lead to disease. And, those in various spiritual traditions wonder if *The Secret* isn't just one more book in a long list that attempts to spiritualize materialism—making greed perfectly acceptable and even spiritually justifiable. In the foreword to the book *Essential Spirituality,* by Roger Walsh, the Dalai Lama says: "In our increasingly materialistic world, we are driven by a seemingly insatiable desire for power and possessions. Yet in this vain striving, we wander even further from inner peace and mental happiness. Despite our pleasant material surroundings, many people today experience dissatisfaction, fear, anxiety, and a sense of insecurity. There seems to be something lacking within our hearts. What we seem to be missing is a proper sense of human spirituality."

Beyond the Secret embraces these concerns, especially the materialistic ones, and attempts to show how the law of attraction can be used along more spiritual lines. Because if there really is a "secret" in life worth discovering, it is not the law of attraction. It is the secret of Spirit, or God, which wants us to attract spiritual, not material, abundance. Finding out what Spirit wants from us and learning how to live a more spiritual life are essential before we even attempt to use the law of attraction. Only then will we put the law of attraction to its greatest use—creating a better, more loving, and compassionate world.

Acknowledgments

What a total blessing this book has been! Spirit guided it in so many ways; it has been truly miraculous! Through Spirit, an amazing group of people were attracted to the process, and I am grateful to show them my warmth and appreciation.

First, to Bettie Youngs, who acted not only as my agent, but as an angel who flew into my life and gave this book the wings it needed to take off. Next, my gratitude and appreciation to Jack Jennings at Hampton Roads Publishing for following his instincts and giving his time and energy to see this book through. Also, thanks to the talented staff at Hampton Roads, including Susan Heim, Tania Seymour, Jane Hagaman, and everyone else who gave their heart and soul to this process.

To the many people who endorsed this book, thank you for your positive feedback. To my parents, Robert and Joan, thanks for your enthusiasm and love. To Will, thanks for nearly two decades of support in helping me launch. To my spiritual teachers, including Michael Robbins, Georgia Lambert, and Michael Miles—your impact on my life has been substantial. To my other teachers, especially those at Loma Linda University, the Institute of Transpersonal Psychology, and those who inspired me through their writings—you all helped shape the ideas in this book.

To my close friends, Linda, Diane, and Greg—the three of you have been there no matter what. To Diane and Stan, thanks for all your wisdom and support these past two years. To my other friends for their encouragement and insight over the years including: Marianne, Gordon and Corinne, Glenda, Nico, Key, Dany, Daniel, Gregg, Glenn, and Bob. To Annie Muller and Richard Schiable, who invested so much in me and are here now only in Spirit. And to Vaylen, my son, my joy, my miracle!

Introduction

My Story

I'm amazed that two decades have passed since I first learned about the law of attraction. You would think that having been gifted with the knowledge of this powerful tool, I would be living quite a different life, one filled with tremendous wealth, health, and happiness. Yet, my life is not that way. What happened? Did I blow it? Did I fail to use the tools I acquired in the right way? Have I sabotaged myself unknowingly for more than twenty-five years? Why is my life in its present state? Despite all of my knowledge about the law of attraction, why might it appear to others as if my life doesn't reflect all of the abundance the universe is supposed to be providing for me?

Actually, the answer is not that complicated. It began with a queasy feeling in my stomach the first time the law of attraction principles were conveyed to me. Something just seemed "off" about the way they were being used. I especially remember the man who joyously affirmed that he wanted to use the law of attraction to manifest a beach house for himself! I have no idea if he succeeded, but I do remember thinking, *Beach house? Is that the best we all can do? Six billion beach houses in the world? Is everyone meant to have a beach house on this Earth?*

As time went by, my puzzlement only deepened. I was raised in the Christian faith, and I took my faith very seriously. As a youth, I immersed myself in Bible stories and took delight in memorizing Biblical verses. By the age of eighteen, I had read the Bible four times through (yep, every word, even all the sections about who begat whom), a different version of it every time. I learned a lot about what the Old Testament (or Torah) and the New Testament had to say about life in Heaven and life on this Earth. So, when I heard about the law of attraction, I wondered how one could use it and still adhere to spiritual principles while trying to get what one wants in the material world!

Of course, even though at times I had difficulty with the notion of the law of attraction, I did manage to use it to manifest quite a bit. The law of attraction *does* work. As I review my life, I am stunned at how many of my wishes have come true. Homes, cars, husbands (two), degrees, a child (who is the joy of my life), my careers (radio, counseling, and writing), and many other items that have come and gone, and come and gone again.

Sometimes I have even been highly amused. I remember the first time I put together a vision board—where you take magazine clippings and create words and images of what you are hoping to manifest. Of the many things I put on the board, I added an ad from a magazine of a singer who had a voice like an angel. I liked to sing, and years later some people did declare how angelic my voice could be. It's just that I didn't expect that one day I would be interviewing on my radio program the same woman in that ad on my board—Cecilia. And, prior to the interview, I was even more amazed when the CD in that ad was sent to me for free! They're powerful stuff, these law of attraction tools.

So, why is my life not more abundant right now, since I have seen many times how the law of attraction can work? Have I been too much of a malcontent? I remember another time in my mid-twenties. I was married to my first husband and sitting in the Jacuzzi near the golf course at our Palm Springs home. (I had two homes back then.) It was a beautiful time of year, quiet and peaceful—and empty! Yes, empty! You see, almost all of the homes around me were unoccupied. Most were second houses to the wealthy elite, who bought homes on or near the golf course for a place to go when they wanted to leave their primary homes to come out and play.

At that time in my life, I was on sabbatical from my counseling career. I had spent a number of years working mainly with troubled youth—runaways, gang kids, homeless kids on the streets, sexually and physically abused children, and teen prostitutes. The clash between the two lifestyles hit me hard. How come many people on the planet didn't have a home at all? Why on Earth should so many people have two homes when they didn't even bother to live in the second one more than a couple of weeks a year?

That day has always stayed with me as a kind of peak experience. Yes, you can use the law of attraction to get whatever you want. But, *should* you? Are some of the things you attempt to manifest really the right, or spiritual, things to wish for? How do you know the difference between a spiritual and a selfish wish? Not surprisingly, my inner turmoil resulted in the eventual rejection of my own wealthy lifestyle. I went back on my prolonged spiritual quest. I spent years exploring in depth the world's major religions. I sat in deep meditation; at one point I was meditating four hours a day for a period of two years. I immersed myself in the wisdom of numerous spiritual writers and read more than a thousand books. I also wrote and taught on spiritual subjects, and I obtained a number of spiritual and psychological degrees.

Despite the fact that during this time I lived at or below a simple middle-class lifestyle, I was generally content. Even when my conditions were meager, I knew that compared to most people on the planet, I still lived in a comparatively wealthy way. At least my basic needs were met. And, as my spiritual practice deepened, I experienced numerous episodes of expanded consciousness, inner bliss, and a steadfast joy no matter what outer circumstances appeared in my life. Then life threw another curve my way, and once again I began to reflect on the law of attraction and how best to use it in the spiritual and material worlds.

It all began when I met a man I was convinced was my one and only soul mate. He was spiritual and mystical, and he lived a simple lifestyle that was a lot like mine. I felt certain we were meant to be together and that the law of attraction had at last brought the right man into my life. There was only one problem. Shortly after meeting me, he also met a woman with a lot of money—and I mean a *lot* of money. It was certainly more money than I had been exposed to in my life at that point, and I had encountered, and even consciously rejected, a fair amount. Because I knew we were "spiritual" people, I felt certain her money would not be an issue. I knew he would adhere to a life of meditation, spiritual study, and monetary simplicity. At the time, I had next to nothing, and so did he. Though we cared about one another, we could barely afford the phone calls to communicate back and forth. (He lived in another country.) To my amazement, the two of them soon ended up together! Apparently, her money had a lot more appeal than my spirituality. Emotionally, I was floored.

For more than a decade after that incident, I searched even harder to reconcile my understanding of the law of attraction as it applied to the spiritual and material worlds. I even made it the topic of one of my PhD dissertations. The title was "Wealth and Spirituality." Confused and frustrated about how to put the two worlds together, I decided to study what every major religion had to say about money in regard to spiritual life. I also studied the lives of extremely wealthy people, both living and deceased. I spent hundreds of hours journaling my beliefs, thoughts, feelings, and assumptions about money, manifestation, and the law of attraction as I understood it at the time. I read countless books on money and how to get what you want through the law of attraction, as well as through other laws and principles. I even trained to become a law of attraction coach. I began writing out my ideas regarding the law of attraction. And I practiced an exercise where I gave myself one billion dollars of fake money to spend. I took a number of months to meditate, read, and learn how on Earth I would use it all wisely and well.

During that intensive period, a number of realizations came to me that I am now happily sharing in this book. One realization arrived by "divine coincidence." While meditating on wealth and spirituality, a symbol emerged in my mind. At first, it appeared as an equal-armed cross. Then, it morphed into two 8s, or infinity symbols, intersecting one another at midpoint. I had never been exposed to this symbol before. One day, while I was sitting in a dissertation class, a female classmate showed up with a picture of exactly the symbol I had envisioned. It was the Buddhist double dorje, their icon for spiritual enlightenment!

How in the world did enlightenment relate to wealth and spirituality? To money? To manifestation? To the law of attraction and its spiritual use? The answers to these questions—arrived at after decades of meditation, study, and application—are in this book. Along with techniques to guide you, this book offers principles that show you how to use the law of attraction along spiritual lines.

Without a clear understanding of these spiritual principles, people can get into serious trouble when using the law of attraction. Just as Jesus in the Christian tradition states, "Seek ye first the kingdom of Heaven, then all things shall be granted unto you," this book advises you to understand the secret of Spirit before you use the law of attraction to manifest what you believe you want and need in your life.

But, be at ease. I have spent decades learning about the spiritual and material worlds, and you will not find me advocating the pursuit of spiritual principles only—just *first*. You will not hear me tell you that to be spiritual you should live an impoverished, monastic lifestyle. For some people, that may be their calling. For most people, it is not. In fact, my dissertation research helped me challenge the assumption that avoiding the material world is a spiritual thing to do. It is often simply the *easier* thing to do. With the gap between the rich and the poor widening all the time, perhaps one of the most spiritual things anyone can do is to manifest wealth in such a way that one is a good custodian of that material abundance in service to others. But then, like Jesus in the desert and Buddha under the bodhi tree, this means you have to face temptation. You have to confront your own strengths and weaknesses around getting whatever you want. Given this opportunity, what will happen to you? Will you hold on to your dignity, integrity, and spiritual values? Or, will you fall, like so many modern-day spiritual teachers and leaders, and sacrifice your values at the altar of self-indulgence and greed?

If there really is a genie in a bottle ready to give you anything you want, do you know what to wish for? And in wishing, will you sell your soul? Only by being tempted will you discover if you pass the test. This is something I realized when I first learned about the law of attraction more than twenty-five years ago. At the time, a spiritual teacher advised our class that come the turn of the century (the era we are living in now), all of humanity would learn about the law of attraction and the secrets of magic, or manifestation, in the universe.

Looking at the vast popularity of *The Secret,* that time is, in fact, now. So, are we truly ready for the genie to come out of the bottle? Are we prepared to handle wisely the power this genie can bestow upon us? Are we spiritually mature enough to use this magical energy in the most constructive way for the good of everyone—not just ourselves? This book is one attempt to offer guidance and to help us be the spiritual masters of the genie and the law of attraction. Only by understanding the principles here can we guide this energy along the right path toward the greatest good for all.

Part I

✦

Spiritual Attraction Ten Basic Steps

It is my sincere hope that this book will be a magical exploration for you! With that in mind, I've devised a ten-step process that will help you use the law of attraction in accordance with Spirit. To make these steps easier to understand and practice, I've further broken down these ten steps into categories that act as acronyms (see the box on the next page), helping to jog your memory about the entire process. I've called them ONE, TWO, and THREE. The ONE stage is the most essential, since these steps put you in touch with Spirit so you can attract what Spirit wants for you. The TWO stage involves listening to Spirit and organizing your thoughts into a clearer mental understanding of what you need to attract. The THREE stage shows you how to turn a thought or idea into a reality. Frequently, this involves working through various emotional and unconscious states in yourself and others that may hinder you from being able to manifest what Spirit desires. An overview of these steps follows:

THE TEN STEPS FOR SPIRITUAL
USE OF THE LAW OF ATTRACTION

ONE Stage: Getting in Touch with Spirit
Orient toward Spirit
Negate the ego
Engage the soul

TWO Stage: Developing a Mental Understanding
Take time to align
Watch and listen
Order your thoughts

THREE Stage: Manifesting What Spirit Wants
Tap into your feelings
Highlight the shadow in others
Remove the shadow from yourself
Execute and **E**asy does it!

For each step, I've given you the basic principles and philosophies for using them. Furthermore, I've provided techniques to help you implement them in effective ways. Some of the techniques may be familiar to you if you already have an understanding of the law of attraction, especially those found in steps six and seven, since that is where the majority of law of attraction books on the market put their focus. After I share these ten steps, I go on to give specific examples of how the law of attraction can be used in various aspects of your life. This includes money, health, relationships, and the world. I hope that the insights, stories, and techniques in this book will not only give you more of what you want, but attract to you what Spirit wants most for you!

The ONE Stage

Getting in Touch with Spirit

Begin any attempt at using the law of attraction by using these three simple steps:

STEP 1

Orient toward Spirit

Before you start wishing for something, invite Spirit into the process. Dedicate yourself toward service. Invite Spirit to guide you to desire only what Spirit also desires for you.

STEP 2

Negate the Ego

Notice all of the ways your ego starts to pout, gets discouraged, reacts, and resists being open to Spirit. Be careful not to judge what happens. Just notice it, and then proceed to the next step.

STEP 3

Engage the Soul

Ask the soul to step in with its healing, wise, and loving powers to assist your ego in becoming more calm, centered, and full of faith, hope, and love. Use the power of the soul to help the ego want what Spirit wants for it.

Chapter 1

Step 1
Orient toward Spirit

If there is one secret truly worth discovering, it is not the secret of the law of attraction. It is the secret of Spirit. True, the law of attraction can bring you whatever you want in life, but as I mentioned before, it won't necessarily bring you what is good for you. Only Spirit understands what you really need and why you are here.

> *Seek to understand what Spirit*
> *wants for you in this life.*

As you will discover, the law of attraction can be used in healthy or unhealthy ways. A child can be attracted to a flame, but the best result is not to put her hand into the fire and get burned. Metaphorically, Spirit can be seen as a divine parent, seeking to guide you into greater wisdom and maturity. And what Spirit ultimately wants for you is simple—to be conscious of the universe.

Spirit also wants you to live an abundant life. But let's be clear on what spiritual abundance is and what it is not. An abundance of Spirit is an abundance of spiritual wisdom and insight. It includes an abundance of spiritual values like patience, love, compassion, maturity, respect, appreciation, intelligence, harmony, inner peace, joy, and a dedication to what is often called the good, the true, and the beautiful.

SPIRIT

Encompasses everything that is!
Everything lives within it and is a part of it.
It has been called "God," "Allah," "The Force,"
and a multitude of other names.
Essentially you are Spirit, and Spirit is you!

Spirit has a fundamental purpose—
to wake you up so you can realize
that ultimately you are Spirit,
and so is everything else around you.
The more you connect with Spirit,
the more you understand that you are here
not to consume, but to contribute.

SPIRITUAL LESSONS ARE EVERYWHERE

Yes, your dharma, or spiritual purpose in life, may involve great monetary wealth. But, then again, it may not! While meditating on wealth and spirituality, I remember one particularly powerful experience. I was reflecting on the times when I had money and when I did not. At the time I was near the ocean. It had just rained, and slowly my attention was drawn to the vast expanse of water in front of me and then to a puddle by the side of the road.

Oceans and puddles. My attention went back and forth between the two. Should I damn the puddle for being so small? Wasn't it serving a purpose? Wasn't it helping to collect a pool of water until the sun could evaporate it? Didn't I have multiple childhood memories of splashing about in puddles? Didn't I remember the delight and laughter of seeing water splash all around me as my boot stomped down into it? Yes, puddles had brought a lot of joy into my life.

As for oceans, having grown up in the Midwest, I always found it a magical experience to head down to Florida to see the vast expanse of water before me: the waves rolling in and out, surfers riding those waves, sea creatures of all kinds inhabiting a whole new universe below. Oceans were always mysterious and enchanting to me, not to mention healing and soothing, which was why I was standing in front of the ocean at that time.

Of course, lakes had always brought a lot of joy to me as well. There were lots of lakes in the Midwest. I loved the water. I liked both sailing and waterskiing, and swimming was always one of my favorite things. Picnics on the grass. Family outings. Those early teenage romantic rendezvous. Except for the chiggers, which could bite you, I never had a memory of a lake I didn't thoroughly adore.

Even water in a glass has a purpose. I don't know about you, but when I am thirsty, it is water in a glass, not water from a lake, ocean, or puddle, I most want to drink. I realized that no matter what form or shape water took, it wasn't about how much water any person did or did not have. It was about the function of the water and how well it was put to use.

And, in that moment I realized that money and all the "stuff" people acquired with it were exactly like water in this world. I came to understand that it wasn't how much any person had or didn't have that mattered. It was the spiritual lessons they were learning from what they possessed and how well they consciously, lovingly, and intelligently managed their possessions. It also mattered that they were capable of sticking to spiritual principles no matter how much wealth or what kind of circumstances they faced in their lives. Perhaps this is why so many spiritual people go through both prosperous and adverse situations. Like the double dorje, they are learning to stand poised at the center of the circle, staying spiritually balanced no matter the outer circumstances of their world.

Spirit Overcomes Fear and Selfish Desire

As you've probably figured out by now, when I talk about using the law of attraction, I am not talking about getting a lot of stuff. Stuff may or may not make you happy. It's just that too often people acquire stuff as a way to avoid their ultimate fear—that stuff may really be all there is in this universe. Just like the stuff of our bodies, one day all that other stuff will disappear as well. The only thing that will remain is Spirit, and even that is difficult for some stuff-driven people to accept and comprehend. Though I have personalized Spirit metaphorically as a divine parent, it really is the vast, all-encompassing force that pervades the universe. As my own mystical experiences have revealed to me, Spirit lives within everything. Nothing can escape it, and everyone is "it" in a very fundamental way.

Understand that Spirit is infinite;
forms are finite.
Spirit is abundant; forms are not.

Thus, those who know Spirit intimately understand beyond a shadow of a doubt that nothing in this universe can be destroyed. Death is an illusion. Whenever anything appears to die, it simply changes shape and form. As Albert Einstein said, "Energy cannot be created or destroyed." This realization radically shifts your experience of death and desire. Though *The Secret* also mentions this Einstein quote, the book fails to illuminate or appreciate how, when you remove the fear of death, you don't desire things in quite the same way.

For starters, you no longer act as a human being who wants to consume everything in sight, leaving nothing of real value for your children and grandchildren in the future. You begin to understand that humans who are only focused on consumption are really like a cancer on this Earth. Just as cancer cells in your body could use the law of attraction to get what they want despite your ultimate demise, humans need to understand that, if they are not careful, they will use the law of attraction in a destructive manner, reaping devastation on the larger world around them.

Of course, even if the law of attraction is used in a selfish way, Spirit will ultimately turn it toward the good. But why make those mistakes? Why set yourself back and misuse the law of attraction instead of applying it in a spiritual way? The difficulty with the law of attraction is that it is entirely neutral. Just as *The Secret* shares, the law of attraction is like a genie in a bottle here to grant your every wish. Often, what you are wishing for is not what Spirit is wishing for you! Just as a child can wish to eat nothing but cookies all day long, what you wish for as an adult may or may not be good for you in the long run. And since the law of attraction is neutral, it doesn't care. It will give you want you want regardless.

Remember the law of attraction is neutral.
Though you can use it to get
whatever you wish for, it doesn't always
give you what Spirit wishes for you!

SPIRIT REVEALS YOUR ULTIMATE DESTINY

So here's the rub: The next time you are busy polishing that lamp so all of your wishes can come true, think twice about what you are doing because the most powerful use of the law of attraction is ultimately to attract to yourself a clear understanding of how to wish! And one of the best wishes you can make is to gain insight into yourself and your spiritual purpose, mission, or ultimate destiny in this world.

Now, I cannot tell you what your ultimate destiny is. Though I can attempt to guide you, only Spirit knows what it is for certain. But I believe Spirit has a fundamental purpose—to wake you up so you can realize that ultimately you are Spirit, and so is everything else around you. Call it enlightenment, self-realization, unity consciousness, oneness, or being filled with the Holy Spirit. It all leads to a quest by which you understand that you are here not to consume but to contribute. You are not here simply to acquire but to give! All that you receive in life is ultimately a gift from Spirit that teaches you to be more loving and aware on this Earth. You might as well face it: No matter how much you use the law of attraction to wish it would not be true, your time on this Earth is finite! How you spend your time here is important. So what on this Earth will you do?

Will you spend your time and energy only trying to obtain your material desires? Especially in the world today, it is possible to attract to yourself a lot of material goods! And, quite frankly, attracting stuff is easy. Just think of all the people you know who have knowingly or unknowingly used the law of attraction to get what they have wanted in life. They may have cars, money, a dream home, the best-looking partner or spouse, good health, and even well-dressed and educated children. On the exterior, their lives look like a dream. Yet, despite all of this, they may also remain lackluster and walk through life half-consciously. To cope, they often medicate themselves with alcohol, Prozac, illegal drugs, adrenaline-rush activities, sexual conquests, and much, much more. Sadly, despite all of their prosperity, too many people in our present society act like empty zombies. Maybe that is why our culture is so increasingly obsessed with horror movies. As a whole, we are trying to wake up to the horror of the empty lives too many people are currently living.

SPIRIT SPARK
Your Spiritual Purpose

If you had to take a guess at your spiritual purpose, what do you think it might be? How clear and defined versus nebulous is this? If you think you already act in alignment with your spiritual purpose, what do you think the next steps might be that Spirit is attracting for you to pursue? If you are out of alignment with your spiritual purpose, when and where will you set aside time to get in touch with the ultimate destiny Spirit has for you? For support, read *The Purpose of Your Life* by Carol Adrienne.

ATTRACT MORE SPIRIT INTO YOUR LIFE

This is why it is so important to attract the things of Spirit no matter what the outer circumstances of your life. Then you will know that if you can stay connected with Spirit, grow in wisdom, and have a heart capable of love, you will remain in a very good mood. Just like Job in the Bible who was stripped of everything and everyone he loved for a while, you will discover it is possible to stay in touch with Spirit for better or worse, in sickness and health, till death do you part, no matter what. You will learn to remain in a state of inner joy and peace whether you take on the role of a Bill Gates or Mother Teresa. My research and life experiences have shown me that people can accomplish this. But I have worked hard and long to know the secret of Spirit in my life. I know this secret of Spirit *really* has the power to free you.

So get busy trying to attract an understanding of the purpose Spirit has for you. But remember that you cannot write that purpose yourself, especially if it is selfish in nature, without paying a price in the end. What does Spirit want most from you? To become conscious and to love. How do you love? By experiencing yourself as connected to everything around you and, as everything and everyone, to learn how to take better care of yourself. Despite the illusion that you are separate from other people, we are all interconnected. Think of a hand: even though you may believe you are only a finger, you are part of the hand nevertheless. As you wake up to this fact, you realize how important it is to care about what happens to the people and the overall planet around you. This is not an easy task. To truly love, you have to understand what everything around you needs to grow and prosper. Try attracting that information to you!

Of course, learning to love everyone and everything around you may seem like an impossible task. That is why it is important to begin in small ways. If you can just learn to love and care for yourself, that alone is a huge accomplishment. If you can also learn to love, care for, and respect your family, neighbors, coworkers, and community—wow! What a wonderful world it would be if we could all do that!

So, why not begin right now to use the law of attraction to help you live a loving and spiritual life? Don't forget to attract to yourself an understanding of just how much you have to offer. That way you will seek to make your life more about contribution, instead of acquisition, as you live from day to day.

Use the law of attraction
to benefit not only yourself,
but everyone around you.

SPIRIT STORY
What Would Spirit Do?

I know a man who lives in Uganda. As a Christian and a deeply spiritual man, he was very concerned regarding the poverty and suffering of people, especially children, around him. Unsure of how to help, he entered into prayer using the following question to guide him, "What would Jesus do?" He decided, despite his meager financial situation, to house in his small home children whose parents had died of AIDS. As his home became more crowded, he again entered into prayer, this time allowing Spirit to guide him to attract the means to establish a school to house and support more children. Then he attracted people in the United States to set up the Children's Heritage Foundation to help him sponsor and care for even more children in need. At the time he got the inspiration to start the school, he had no idea how to make it happen. He simply made the commitment to begin. And no matter what the outer circumstances, he stayed in touch with Spirit, praying to God and his spiritual mentor (Jesus) to guide him to find ways to establish, build, and maintain his school. What a beautiful example of the spiritual use of the law of attraction and how any of us can use the law of attraction to accomplish all the good we are meant to.

ORIENT TOWARD SPIRIT
Key Insights

1. Seek to understand what Spirit wants for you in this life.

2. Understand that Spirit is infinite; forms are finite. Spirit is abundant; forms are not.

3. Remember the law of attraction is neutral. Though you can use it to get whatever you wish for, it doesn't always give you what Spirit wishes for you!

4. Use the law of attraction to benefit not only yourself, but everyone around you.

Chapter 2

Step 2
Negate the Ego

All of us have an ego—that part of ourselves that is totally focused on our needs, desires, thoughts, feelings, talents, drama, or wants in the world. In and of itself, the ego is not a problem. Each of us needs to pay some attention to ourselves. We all need to master the skills that help us feed and clothe our bodies, manage our emotions constructively, and handle our problems with greater skill. Only as we learn to do this can we drop our attention from our own issues and focus on the needs of others whom we are meant to serve (children, parents, partners, employers, employees, Spirit, and all of life itself).

> *The ego is that part of us that is totally focused*
> *on its own wants and desires.*

When people are overly stuck in their egos, they can become energy vampires to everyone around them. The psychological word for them is *narcissist*. A narcissist doesn't know how to step out of his own world or point of view to understand and see clearly the reality of others. In Greek mythology, Narcissus spies a reflection of himself in a pool of water and spends the rest of his life gazing at it, contemplating how handsome and wonderful he is. Sadly, it is difficult to get the ego to move beyond its constant focus on itself. Like Narcissus gazing into the pool for hours on end, ego-driven individuals don't understand how many positive opportunities move by them, because they simply don't know how to pay attention to anyone or anything else other than themselves.

Ego as Narcissist

Why certain people become narcissistic is not easy to comprehend. When the self-esteem movement came into being, it asserted people may become egotistical to compensate for the bruised and damaged reflections they received of themselves as children. If eventually they receive positive mirroring from others, they learn to love and respect themselves and lessen their insatiable needs for attention, which they attempt to achieve through either constructive or destructive means.

As a therapist, my role was often one of trying to give the positive feedback that their parents, through a lack of understanding or skill, failed to offer them.

But from a spiritual perspective we need to do more than build up self-esteem in others. We need to stop feeding the ego altogether. This is because frequently the ego doesn't know when to quit. It won't stop playing what I call the See Me game long enough to see what others are going through. The ego plays this See Me game because it constantly craves attention. During certain stages in life (childhood and life crises, for example), it is natural to be overly absorbed in your own issues, but beyond a certain point this is not healthy growth.

Learn how the ego constantly seeks attention
by playing the See Me game.

BASIC ELEMENTS OF THE EGO

The ego is based on a sense of separation, and it causes you to feel different from everyone around you. A person with a healthy ego knows she is similar to others and seeks points of connection with others by way of the soul. A person with an unhealthy ego emphasizes how special or unique she is compared to others, either in her gifts or her deficiencies. The ego is also known as the "mask," "persona," or "personality" of an individual. Often the ego is said to be composed of the following three elements:

- **Mind:** This is the "thinking" part of the ego. It helps provide the reason why things happen in an abstract or logical way. It also allows us to formulate ideas and to figure out how to make them work in the world.

- **Feelings:** Nonrational feelings help us get a "sense" of things. At a basic level, they help us decide if something is pleasurable or painful. On a broader level, they break down into a variety of states: anger, sorrow, jealousy, happiness, confusion, et cetera. When we express our feelings to others, instead of just experiencing them privately, they "move out" and become emotions.

- **Body:** This is simply the physical body, with all of its parts, organs, and systems. Some people include the energy, or vital, body here as well.

"See me!" Like a vacuum cleaner, the person stuck in his ego will suck others into paying attention to his continual dramas. It's bad enough that narcissists are stuck on themselves. Beyond this, narcissists want you to be stuck on them, too. There are many ways the See Me game is played. The "put-down" approach of the See Me game goes something like this: "See how powerful, loving, intelligent, beautiful, devoted, organized, rich, and successful I am compared to you." On the flip side, the "I'm too helpless" approach goes something like this: "See how difficult, full of pain, abusive, broke, chaotic, and horrible my life is next to how yours looks."

Now, some people *are*, in fact, more powerful, loving, intelligent, rich, beautiful, and so forth than others. Though everyone is equal in Spirit, the fact is that in this world there will always be people who are better or worse in some areas than you. And some people are, in fact, suffering horribly. As a counselor, I was exposed to some very heart-wrenching cases of abuse and pain. It was difficult not to feel angry or sad regarding this suffering, especially when it involved children. No child (or human being for that matter) should be subjected to any form of abuse. But, the egotistical person lives in a very self-absorbed world and is obsessed with discovering how well he is measuring up compared to you. If a person stuck in the ego feels superior to you, he is likely to flaunt that superiority in an arrogant manner. If that person feels inferior to you, he is likely to demean himself, acting as if he could never be worthy of you, health, or happiness, no matter what.

All of this is important in understanding the law of attraction because, as I mentioned before, the law of attraction is neutral. It will give you what you want regardless of whether you are focused on Spirit or your ego! Both spiritual and narcissistic people are capable of acquiring many of the same things. How do you know if someone who possesses beauty, wealth, intelligence, or power is coming from ego or Spirit? Simple. If someone comes from Spirit, the goal will be to acquire these things for the purpose of helping others. If someone comes from ego, they will only want the stuff of this world for the purpose of calling attention to themselves.

Outgrowing the Ego

When I studied the lives of wealthy people, I was especially interested in this distinction. I had already decided that it was perfectly all right for some people to have great wealth. What mattered was if they were prospering others with the wealth they possessed. I also came to understand that anyone with a lot of money becomes a custodian, whether they like it or not, of a vision. The money and other resources they acquire should ultimately fuel that vision. If that vision is in alignment with Spirit, these vast resources will help all of us to live in a better world. If that vision is focused only on the ego, then none of us will fare too well. This is how I came to understand that money is not really the problem—ego is. So, whether you like it or not, you have to confront a fundamental truth:

To grow spiritually,
you must outgrow your ego,
minimizing its needs and demands.

Certainly, the ego doesn't want to hear that! The ego wants what it wants when it wants it. Like a two-year-old having a temper tantrum, the ego doesn't understand that maybe others have needs, too. Herein lies the danger regarding how the law of attraction can be used by the ego. While the ego is busy satisfying its own desires, it may be neglecting how adversely it is impacting those around it.

For example, in the 1980s movie *Wall Street,* Michael Douglas portrayed a businessman who announced, "Greed is good." Many executives of top corporations such as Enron couldn't have agreed more. Jeffrey Skilling of Enron prided himself on his vast intellect, and he used it to manipulate other people out of their money to profit his own bank account and those of other Enron executives. Skilling was also a big fan of *The Selfish Gene,* a book I was required to read during my undergraduate years at Michigan State University. At only twenty years old, I understood that the selfish gene or ego lives all around us. Fortunately, there are plenty of examples of how Spirit and the unselfish impulse exist on this Earth, too!

At the same time in the 1980s, I remember reading a bumper sticker that was very popular: "He who dies with the most toys wins!" This is exactly what the ego wants—to acquire as much as it can, no matter who suffers in the end. Later, that bumper sticker was countered by one that declared, "He who dies with the most toys still dies!" Though this version causes one to pause, it doesn't totally express the importance of remembering what kind of legacy you will leave when you die. When you've left this Earth, will people be thankful to distribute the wealth you left them, while being happy that you are gone? Or, would they gladly give away any inherited material goods from you if they could have just one more day to enjoy your presence?

The point is that this planet only becomes hell on Earth if the law of attraction is used to feed the ego and its narcissistic greed. And, though it is always a good thing to be grateful for what you have in life as *The Secret* suggests, simply being grateful for what you have is not enough if you are only using the law of attraction to satisfy the desires of your ego. After all, plenty of egotistical people are very grateful for their ability to serve mainly themselves.

This is why motive is so important when you begin to wish for something and why it is essential to align with Spirit in order to understand what you should really be wishing for. Remember, Spirit ultimately wants you to discover your interconnection with everything and everyone around you. It wants the ego to expand its point of view and to include others in the picture when it engages in the wishing process.

SPIRIT SPARK
The Unselfish Gene!

Take a moment and consider, who are the people who have inspired you the most? People who managed to take something from you—leaving you spiritually, mentally, emotionally, and financially bankrupt? Or, people who left you in a better place, even if they did so by teaching you a few hard lessons that forced you to grow in a more positive direction? I remember a scene from the musical play *Les Misérables* where an act of charity from a priest (a gift of silver tableware) to the convict Jean Valjean stirred so much emotion within Valjean that he completely changed his life. From that point on, he dropped his hatred and dedicated himself to doing good. Not all acts of charity have to be this dramatic. If you pay attention, you will notice simple acts of kindness going on all the time around you. In fact, by putting your attention on the "unselfish gene," you might be amazed at how much kindness exists in the world if you open yourself up to noticing and attracting it.

SPIRIT HAS THE LAST WORD

Though it is best for you to grow naturally into the realization that you need to outgrow your ego, if you don't eventually learn this, Spirit may have the last word. This is difficult for many people who use the law of attraction to understand. They have been ingrained with the notion that, no matter what, they are entitled to get whatever they want. If they don't get it, they assume it is because they are not wishing hard enough. Thus, they will apply law of attraction techniques to push even harder to manifest their desires. Sadly, it doesn't occur to them that maybe these desires are being thwarted by a higher power or force beyond their own egos, which leads to the following insight:

If you hang on to your ego for too long,
Spirit will block its desires;
any attempts by the ego to use
the law of attraction will now be in vain.

No matter what the ego desires, what Spirit wants for you holds more power. Ultimately, Spirit will get its way. The ego will try to counter this by saying, "Oh, no. I can find a way to have whatever I want." But, Spirit is infinite and far more aware than ego consciousness, and it knows better. This is why learning to surrender to Spirit whenever you wish for something becomes so essential in the manifestation process.

Think about it. Review in your mind a time when you attempted to attract something and failed. If you didn't slip deeper into ego tendencies by holding on to the anger and bitterness this generated, chances are something good came out of the loss. Maybe you learned some valuable lessons that caused you to change your attitude and behaviors, or you launched into a different direction that ended up giving you more than you could ever have hoped for. Learning these lessons of Spirit gives the ego a necessary dose of both humility and hope.

After all, the love of your life may never return, but you might just learn to be a more loving person. Your finances may never hit a high level, but you can still learn to love and better care for the simple things in life. An illness may even take someone you love away from you, but that person's spiritual essence can still live and breathe within your heart. These are examples of attracting spiritual values that help you make something rewarding out of life no matter what is attracted to you.

So, is it really possible to teach your ego to minimize i tendencies so it will happily surrender to Spirit? Or will your (and fight to get its own way until its dying breath? If you are (to feed your ego only, Spirit might just attract some painfu. ....ons your way to help illuminate you and encourage you to change. Since you are reading this book, having to go through these kinds of painful lessons is less likely because you are probably already inclined toward living a spiritual life. Most likely you want to give birth to your spiritual self and to have peace of mind about the life you have lived in the end. But, even if you are on a spiritual quest, it is still important to remain aware of how your own ego can disrupt your higher aspirations and attempt to use the law of attraction in a selfish way. I hope the lessons here will help you safely discern the ways your ego might attempt to trick you. They will show you how to stop your ego from winning so you can use the law of attraction in a truly spiritual way.

SPIRIT STORY
Sticks and Stones

Kevin always wanted to be a professional musician. Though he had talent, his father worried that he would have trouble making a living in such a difficult field. Instead of expressing his concerns in a soulful way, Kevin's father ridiculed his guitar playing even though others felt Kevin had real skill. Kevin fought back his disappointment by reminding himself of the chant he had learned as a child, "Sticks and stones may break my bones, but words will never hurt me." But this phase only hid a deeper truth reflected in another saying, "Sticks and stones may break my bones, but words can break my heart." Once Kevin's heart had been broken, he lost confidence in himself and ironically became overly critical of others in the music field. At times he even delighted in trashing other people's talent, going so far as to ridicule and humiliate them when they then acted hurt by his barbs. When he likewise became a father, his daughter decided she wanted to be a singer. One day, after he made a particularly sarcastic comment to her about the field, his daughter broke down into tears. Suddenly Kevin remembered his own pain and disappointment as a youth at being discouraged from entering a profession he loved. He saw how his anger and bitterness were a cover-up for his own hurt. Seeing his daughter's pain finally opened his heart up again. In time he even embraced her dream, helping her to find a way to make it come true if that was what she truly desired.

Negate the Ego
Key Insights

1. The ego is that part of us that is totally focused on its own wants and desires.

2. Learn how the ego constantly seeks attention by playing the See Me game.

3. To grow spiritually, you must outgrow your ego, minimizing its needs and demands.

4. If you hang on to your ego for too long, Spirit will block its desires; any attempts by the ego to use the law of attraction will now be in vain.

Chapter 3

Step 3
Engage the Soul

One of the main reasons the ego continues to exist is because it lives in fear. And, the one thing the ego fears most is loss. Loss of control, image, status, beauty, power, intelligence, people, possessions, money, health—even the loss of life itself—keeps the ego in a constant state of trying to protect and preserve itself. Since Spirit has as its essential purpose dissolving all protective barriers, Spirit is one of the greatest threats there is to the ego. That's why the soul, which is mainly love, is needed to help cushion Spirit as it shatters the protective boundaries of the ego.

Your soul is the bridge
between ego and Spirit.

Choosing Love

The love of the soul and the fear of the ego cannot coexist. This is because love expands, while fear contracts. Love opens, while fear closes. Love lives in the present, while fear lives in regret of the past or anxiety over the future. In short, the two counter each other in every way. At the most basic level, fear is simply a sensorial response that asks you to pay attention, to be aware of what is happening around and within you. When you don't pay attention, irrational fear steps in. You fail to learn from your mistakes, and you no longer focus on the here and now. You may even repel something that Spirit is trying to attract your way. You can also get overly aggressive in an attempt to attract something even if you are not meant to have it.

As you align with Spirit through the love of the soul, fear erodes. You stay open to receiving what you are meant to have. Even if you don't understand the purpose beneath what you are receiving at the time, there is a sense that it will all work out in the end. The result is an inner feeling of calm and well-being that emerges as you learn to trust in Spirit and let your ego go.

Whenever you sense fear emerging, call upon the power of the soul. Attempt to move beyond what your ego believes it needs and wants. Use love to help your ego shift from fear into faith. Maybe your ego will receive what it longs for. But even if it doesn't, help your ego to trust that no matter what happens, if it cultivates spiritual abundance, the end result can still be good.

THE NATURE OF THE SOUL

The soul acts as the bridge between the seemingly separated world of the ego and the all-inclusive world of Spirit. In many philosophical systems, it has been connected to consciousness as well. Although, in a sense, everything has a soul because everything is linked to Spirit, a truly soulful person possesses certain spiritual qualities. These include:

Authenticity · Sincerity · Love · Joy
Understanding · Compassion · Detachment
Divine Indifference · Humor · Serenity
Humility · Courage · Patience · Wisdom
Perseverance · Service · Inclusiveness
Sharing · Intuition · Responsibility

The soul uses the law of attraction to bring these qualities into the ego. These qualities also emerge more as the ego becomes aware of the vastness of Spirit, while at the same time its sense of discrete importance diminishes. As it becomes "soul-infused," the ego increasingly seeks to simply play its part well in relation to everything around it so that it can make a contribution to others.

Recognizing Love

What is love? Over the years, I have come to understand that much of what people identify as love is nothing of the sort. It is codependency, lust, neediness, addiction, and the ego's constant desire for attention. Sadly, the overwhelming majority of television shows, movies, and music really reflects a spiritual sickness in our world. Using the acronym ILL, what most people are saying is "I lack love" and not "I have love." It is important to understand the difference.

How do you know if someone has love to give? Here are some brief guidelines:

1. Loving people are joyful and grateful despite the outer circumstances that have been attracted into their lives.

2. Loving people strive for understanding and actively seek to be an agent of compassion and wisdom in the world.

3. Loving people tend to experience a greater measure of inner peace and are more often filled with well-being because they are more consistently connected to Spirit by way of their souls.

4. Loving people are able to face life in a positive and courageous way and attempt to overcome any difficulties life brings them with poise, grace, and a pro-active stance.

Loving people also increasingly understand the difference between using the law of attraction in a spiritual versus an egotistical way. Spirit desires that you contribute and love. It constantly seeks to attract to you the experiences and lessons that will free your ego from its selfish grip, even if at times those experiences are painful.

The function of your soul is to expand your capacity to love.

Please understand that Spirit does not want you to suffer. It actually wants you to suffer *less!* It knows that not everything the ego wants to acquire and attract is good for it in the long run. It is not good to indulge in behaviors that will ultimately hurt yourself and others. In my research on wealth and spirituality and in my practice counseling others, too often I have found this to be true. Individuals who have been very, very successful at attracting much of what they want in this life materially may still be very miserable people.

Does that make it bad to want the big house, the fancy sports car, the life of luxury, the good-looking partner, the fame and success?

No, no, and *no!* All of these things are fine and good. You see, it's not what you acquire in life; it's your motivation for acquiring it. Remember that the law of attraction is neutral. It will bring you what you want, even if it's not good for you. Spirit is not neutral. The soul, as an agent of Spirit, wants only to attract to you that which will increase the odds of you becoming a loving, compassionate, wise, and spiritual person.

Since the ego is very tricky, it will attempt to fool you. Like a two-year-old, it will resist the efforts of the soul. Remember, the ego wants what it wants when it wants it. If the ego doesn't listen, Spirit will guide the soul to act as a divine parent and restrict the ego's desires somehow. But why go down that route? Why not learn to transform your ego's selfish desires and wants?

Your soul will consistently attempt
to purify your ego's motives
regarding what it wants to attract.

Living Love

Of course, some things seem as if they are obviously good to wish for. It's reasonable to believe that the soul wants you to have good health, a loving partner, well-adjusted children, and enough material abundance to live a happy and spiritual life. If, as you serve others, such blessings come your way, then be a wise and generous custodian of them. Enjoy the homes, cars, clothes, good health, and vacation retreats, but remain unattached. Remember, you do not need these things to feel good about who you really are.

Again, the ego wants to play the See Me game. It wants others to see how rich, powerful, beautiful, successful, and wonderful it is. It needs stuff like fancy cars, rich and famous friends, good-looking partners, and huge homes to help ensure its outer image, its facade of feeling good. The soul couldn't care less about these outer trappings except for how they are useful in service. That's why soulful people can be content with or without all of these wonderful outer displays of money and power. They simply use the power of the soul to learn to be loving and wise no matter what outer circumstances life throws them into.

Think of some of the great spiritual leaders of our time who moved in and out of all aspects of life—rich and poor, sick and well, soulful and despicable—while still retaining their values and spiritual center. The Dalai Lama, Mother Teresa, Nelson Mandela, Martin Luther King Jr., Gandhi—all of them could have simply focused on collecting material goods. Instead, they were more interested in living according to spiritual principles, becoming an example of the following:

> *The soul wants you to treat*
> *whatever you attract*
> *with care, respect, and love.*

Now, you don't have to be like one of these spiritual leaders. You have your own ultimate destiny, whether it be in finance, religion, politics, education, the arts, science, law, or any other field. Just be sure that in whatever profession you choose, you take good care of what you acquire—be it your body, your clothes, your children, your partner, your work, or your friends. Appreciate what you have. Be grateful. And don't forget to clean, mend, respect, honor, and enjoy fully whatever or whoever comes into your life.

Unfortunately, we live in a society that does far too little of this. In many ways, the law of attraction is wreaking havoc all around. Too many people are now overly concerned with simply indulging their wishes. They barely slow down to appreciate and acknowledge what they have. For this reason we have become a society of breadth and little depth. Everything, including soul values, has become increasingly disposable. Naturally, those who indulge like this think that the party will go on forever. They forget that even though there is an abundance of Spirit, there is not an abundance of form.

If we don't treat what we attract to us in a loving way, why should the soul give us more? After all, you wouldn't give money to someone who consistently abused it and threw it away. You wouldn't loan your car to someone who only wanted to be reckless with it. Only if your self-esteem is shattered would you let your body, emotions, and thoughts be abused by another individual. You would say *no* to all of this; not *yes!* And, despite what some who use the law of attraction assert—and what *The Secret* tries to dissuade you from believing— "no" can be a very powerful word; so can the phrase "don't want"! It's a shame that at times *The Secret* almost tries to make you feel guilty about applying this phrase.

SPIRIT SPARK
Is There a Price for Wishing?

In his amazing documentary *An Inconvenient Truth,* Al Gore gives us a sobering look at the high price humanity is paying for its excessive focus on consumption and attracting things—like an overdependence on oil and other energy sources—that are no longer good for our environment. Due to overpopulation and massive consumption of the Earth's resources, we are increasingly depleting our world. We may even be causing the premature demise of the human race. Because of this, there is a growing movement to simplify our lifestyles. As Melissa Etheridge declared in the recent Live Earth worldwide concert, it is time for us to stop our constant need to consume. In short, we need to start "wishing for less" so we can focus on quality over quantity. We can also benefit if we slow down our lives so we can deepen our relationships with others, have more time for spiritual practice, and truly learn to care for one another.

<hr>

Only Love

Now, not everyone who uses the law of attraction has the same viewpoint regarding using "no" and "don't want." Some encourage you to look at what you *don't* want to get clearer about what you *do* want. But here is another "secret" that I will teach you that goes way beyond the compare and contrast approach of learning what you don't and do want in this world. Just as there is something called the law of attraction, there is something equally as valuable known as the law of repulse. The soul uses both with regard to your ego. Like a good parent, the soul will attract to you what it wishes to help you grow spiritually. It will also repel, or rip away, from you anything that is hindering your spiritual growth and success. Ironically, the ego often experiences this "repulsing" process as suffering and pain. The soul knows better. It knows that some things it takes away from you are for a higher good and that the pain you are now in is nothing compared to the pain you would feel later if you don't start taking a higher path.

Just one day before writing these words, I was in a parking lot preparing to drop off a letter. A woman came out of a store with her two young daughters, who seemed to be around the ages of four and five. All the way from the store to the car, the older girl was screaming bloody murder because she wanted some stickers from the store and her mother refused to get them for her. The girl proceeded to throw the biggest tantrum I have ever seen a child throw in my life. (Having worked with young children professionally, I have seen quite a few!) With amazing grace and patience, the mother consistently said, "No." She soothed her daughter with words like, "You must be very tired. You can't have the stickers, but you can go swimming in the pool when we get home."

Because of the intensity of the tantrum and all of the stares the mother was getting from other people, including myself, I kept wondering if she would break her resolve and give in to her daughter's fierce demands. If she had, the little girl would have learned a very unfortunate lesson: that she could get whatever she wanted if she was loud, abusive, and obnoxious enough. Instead, with a lot of skill, her mother stayed firm, loving, and unwavering in her response to her daughter's tantrum. And the mother used the power of her soul to teach the little girl something very valuable: Sometimes we are not meant to get what we believe we want in the world, such as temporary stuff like stickers. Sometimes, the soul wants other lessons to "stick" to us, like humility and respect for others.

As I have demonstrated, the ego will act very much like this little girl at times. If it doesn't get what it wants, it will persist and even use the law of attraction to attempt to get its way no matter what. Thankfully, the soul is much wiser. It represents a higher state of consciousness and has a larger perspective of what will make us really happy in this world. By following its guidance, the ego increases the odds of allowing the soul fuller expression so that at the end of life, the dying process will be filled with peace and a joyful conscience instead of guilt, anxiety, disappointment, anger, despair, fear, and doubt.

SPIRIT STORY
Detachment and Divine Indifference

George had struggled with his son's attention deficit disorder (ADD) for years. Though at one level he knew better, he found it irritating that a sophisticated and highly accomplished man like himself had a son who could be so unfocused and scattered. George prayed for the ability to accept his son for who he was, but it wasn't working; that is, until George learned about detachment and divine indifference. Healthy detachment, he discovered, allows people to see and accept a situation for what it is. By letting go of judgment and expectations, they are better able to handle life in a caring way. Divine indifference helps individuals surrender their ego attachment to an outcome. They cultivate faith that all things can work out for the best if they only let go and let God! George realized that he had made an ego investment in his son being a certain way. He decided to detach from this expectation, which allowed him to relax more around his boy. And as George cultivated faith that God had a divine plan for his son, George's heart opened up as well. He even saw that divine plan already manifesting through his own subtle transformation. In short, George was learning to be a more soulful individual. Not surprisingly, as other people found George to be more patient, accepting, and compassionate, they liked being around him more. This made him a better boss, husband, parent, and friend. It helped George understand that learning about detachment and divine indifference through the gift of his son had been worth it!

ENGAGE THE SOUL
Key Insights

1. Your soul is the bridge between ego and Spirit.

2. The function of your soul is to expand your capacity to love.

3. Your soul will consistently attempt to purify your ego's motives regarding what it wants to attract.

4. The soul wants you to treat whatever you attract with care, respect, and love.

Chapter 4

ONE Techniques

STEP 1

Orient toward Spirit

**Before you start wishing for something,
invite Spirit into the process. Dedicate yourself
to service. Invite Spirit to guide you to desire
only what Spirit also desires for you.**

Orienting toward Spirit doesn't have to be difficult. On the simplest level you can just invite Spirit (or God) into the process and say something like, "Not my will, but thine be done" (to use a phrase from the Christian Bible). Saying something like this reminds you that, despite your firm convictions, you may not always know what is best, helping you to stay open to what Spirit may be attracting to you instead. The wisdom of this kind of uncertainty is reflected in a famous quote from Abraham Lincoln: "Sir, my concern is not whether God is on our side. My great concern is to be on God's side." In addition to the above, the following practices also help keep you oriented toward Spirit:

Find Your Spiritual Mentors. Start by making a list of the various spiritual teachers who most inspire you. These teachers may or may not be a part of a religious tradition. They may or may not be people you directly know. They may also be family members, friends, or individuals who work in a variety of fields. Or they may be people or beings who are no longer in a physical body in this world. Whoever they are, make a list of them and write down specifically why they inspire you. Then keep that list handy so you can be inspired anytime you need to.

Engage in Your Spiritual Practice. Now take a look at the spiritual practices that you are most attracted toward using. They may include attending a church, synagogue, or mosque. Or they may involve prayer, meditation, art, music, or dance. Maybe they involve traveling to a sacred space or to a place in nature where you feel you can communicate with Spirit. Whatever practice works for you, use it and then implement the law of attraction to bring to you a revelation of what Spirit most wants for you right now. This revelation may come about through the intuition. Or it could happen during a conversation with someone else. It might also come in a more dramatic way through an opportunity appearing that you had not considered before which finally opens the door to something you have always hoped for. Whatever it is, stay open to spiritual guidance so you can increasingly understand the best path for your life. Then, do your best to pledge yourself more fully to traveling down that path in a conscious, loving, and willing way.

SPIRIT SPARK
The Wisdom of Uncertainty

Susan Jeffers, a best-selling author, gives excellent guidelines for embracing uncertainty in her book, *Embracing*

Uncertainty: Breakthrough Methods for Achieving Peace of Mind When Facing the Unknown. She shares how "a deep acceptance that life is uncertain opens the door to a powerful way of living." As we give up looking for guarantees and embrace uncertainty, excitement and new possibilities open up to us. Instead of always thinking that we have to be the directors of our life shows, we can take "a good seat in the theater and let the story unfold." Her words demonstrate why orienting toward Spirit is important. We must also remember to remain uncertain at an ego level so we can stay open to what Spirit might want for us.

STEP 2

Negate the Ego

Notice all of the ways your ego starts to pout,
gets discouraged, reacts, and resists being open to Spirit.
Be careful not to judge what happens.
Just notice it and then proceed to the next step.

One of the best ways to notice that ego is operating in your life is to pay attention to how much it plays the See Me game. You can start by making a list of the things that you most cherish about yourself in the way of talents, looks, accomplishments, and skills. You can also make a second list of trouble spots, including problems, perceived character flaws, and wounds you feel you still suffer from. Whatever you list, notice if there is a tendency to feel really special because of it. Examples might include, "I'm so much better at this talent than anyone else." Or, "I suffer so much more than other people around me do." These statements are different from simple acknowledgments like, "I feel grateful that I have this talent or gift in life." Or, "I am really struggling with this difficulty right now." It's one thing to simply acknowledge what is, which can be healthy. It's another to feel special, separate, and all alone in the process.

After you make your list, notice how many times in a day, week, or month you attempt to get others to notice your "special" assets or liabilities. Also, see how you do this in your private thoughts. Through this exercise, attempt to understand how much your ego rules your life. If you discover your ego is playing the See Me game a great deal, consider that you may have some major work to do.

One way to diminish the ego is to expand your consciousness in the following ways. Regarding every accomplishment or problem you feel you possess, begin to think about and acknowledge all of the other people who may have similar accomplishments or problems like yours. For example, if you pride yourself on your intelligence, attempt to appreciate that same quality in someone else. You might even remember that there are different kinds of intelligence. There is the intelligent facility of being able to remember all kinds of details and facts accurately and well. There is emotional intelligence, which includes knowing how to interact with other people in a skillful and harmonious way. And there is creative intelligence, which is the capacity to be open and receptive to all kinds of new ideas. Whatever your kind of intelligence, just be sure to notice the intelligence others possess. The same could be said for any other quality (beauty, financial savvy, creativity, and so on).

As for any difficulties you may be struggling with, use a similar process to expand your awareness of how others may be suffering the same way you are. Consider all of the people on this Earth who may be searching for food, clothing, or shelter. Recognize how many other people may feel lonely, have a disease or disability, or are trying to cope with a major loss of some kind. If you can, notice at least one person a day who may feel as lost, afraid, angry, or hurt as you. As you do this, allow your heart to open up and soften, since you now know you are not alone in your pain on this Earth. You might even want to orient toward Spirit and ask that as you seek to heal your own suffering, you become a more effective agent for uplifting and healing the suffering of others.

SPIRIT SPARK
Five Wishes

Today is your lucky day! Your genie has arrived and you are being given five wishes! Quick, make your list! Be as sincere as you possibly can. Don't censor what you are wanting, or worry if what you are wishing for comes from Spirit or your ego. Once you are finished, evaluate what you see. How many of your wishes are centered only on the desires of your ego versus being of service to others?

STEP 3

Engage the Soul

Ask the soul to step in with its healing, wise, and loving powers to assist your ego in becoming more calm, centered, and full of faith, hope, and love. Use the power of the soul to help the ego want what Spirit wants for it.

In many ways, the soul is like a loving and compassionate friend you can speak to wherever and whenever you feel so inclined. Learning to speak to this wise counselor can be a very healing and nurturing exercise. If you have trouble relating to the soul because it seems too abstract, consider communicating with a spiritual teacher, saint, or being such as an angel. Whatever you choose, find a way to connect with the soul. See this exercise as a way to teach your ego how to relax, let go, and develop more faith and confidence in what the soul is trying to reveal to it about what Spirit wants.

If you like, you can turn this into a more formal dialogue between the ego and the soul. Try putting a line down the middle of a page, creating two columns. In one column, write the conversation of the ego, which frequently comes out as questions or concerns posed to the soul. In the other column, put all of the responses the soul offers. Be careful not to censor the process. Just let your intuition and imagination carry you through. Later you can analyze what you have written. For now, simply be spontaneous and creative, letting whatever needs to emerge to do so.

If a line down the middle of the page seems too cumbersome for you, you can also simply draw a line in between paragraphs where the ego switches over to the soul. You can even set it up as if it were a movie script.

Sample Movie Script Dialogue

Ego: I really need to make sure I have this amount of success and money by the end of the year.
Soul: I understand, but there are some other steps that may have to happen first.

Ego: What do you mean? Can't you see how urgent this process is? I need to have this happen sooner, not later.
Soul: Yes, but you have made these assertions before and sabotaged them. I need you to become more conscious of the various obstacles you put onto the path so you can overcome them. Then your success will be more assured in the end; not to mention that you will have more wisdom and greater peace of mind overall.

Ego: Well, if you say so, but I'm still not too sure about all of this.
Soul: I understand, but if you let me guide you step-by-step, you will begin to see the wisdom of what I am trying to do as we proceed.

Hopefully in this small example you can see how many things can come out of engaging in such a dialogue, including helping your ego gain insight, comfort, clearer guidance, and more!

Spirit Spark
Before You Wish

If you are seeking to use the law of attraction in a more soulful way, then the following questions are good to consider before you wish for anything.

1. Will what I am wishing for serve others, not just myself?

2. By acquiring what I seek will I increase the odds that I will grow into a more loving, conscious, compassionate, and wise person?

3. In getting what I wish for will I be able to help others grow and become better people?

4. What do I most need to manifest in my life right now to serve my highest and best good and the good of those around me?

5. How should my life be reorganized and reprioritized so I am more in alignment with what Spirit wants for me?

6. What areas of my life are most neglected right now and need my attention so I can make more space for Spirit in my life?

7. Who or what can help me remove any blocks that are keeping my highest and best good from flowing more directly to me and through me?

The TWO Stage

Developing a
Mental Understanding

After you have sufficiently oriented your ego toward Spirit, follow these three steps to help you understand more clearly what Spirit wants for you:

STEP 4

Take Time to Align

Starting with an attitude of surrender, align the three aspects of your ego—thoughts, feelings, and body—with Spirit. Take time to make sure each part is committed and willing to make a contribution.

STEP 5

Watch and Listen

After aligning the ego with Spirit, enter into meditation. As you meditate, be attentive and curious about discovering what Spirit most wants you to attract into your life at this time.

STEP 6

Order Your Thoughts

Create soul stories so you are more likely to receive various ideas, intuitions, and insights from Spirit. Then order your thoughts so you can carry out the wishes of Spirit.

Chapter 5

ⓘⓈⓈ~

Step 4
Take Time to Align

In *The Secret,* the author outlines three steps for getting what you want: ask, believe, and receive. These steps are based on the premise that to have whatever you want, you simply need to ask for it, believe you can have it, and be willing to receive it. But, as I am demonstrating to you, at times getting what you ask for may not be that good for you.

Someone could easily argue with me and ask, "Why shouldn't I get whatever I want? What is wrong with people enjoying health, great wealth, and happiness in this life?" In an ideal world, I agree it would be great if no one had to know the pain of illness, poverty, or emotional discontent. I am all for living on a planet where people learn only through positive experiences. It would be a pleasure if everyone's ego would easily surrender and embrace spiritual values like charity, simplicity, goodwill, and love. Then everyone would automatically benefit from whatever was wished for on a personal level, and it really would be Heaven here on Earth.

It's just that too often the ego is more stubborn than perhaps even the soul would like. For how many thousands of years have ethical codes like the Ten Commandments been in existence, but are still not followed by the masses of people? Buddhism, Taoism, Hinduism, Confucianism, and Islam all have their ethical precepts as well. These codes are not in place simply because some "God out there" somewhere wants you to behave or else! They signify that if you willingly follow the basics, you can be on your way to living a life of integrity, dignity, and inner peace.

Why Ego Should Surrender

The irony, and perhaps even the tragedy, is that the ego typically only learns the hard way. How many people have you known or heard about who only became more loving and compassionate after they nearly died from a fatal illness or lost everything they owned? Abusive people, for example, rarely give up their abusive behaviors since they get far too many goodies (things they want) from intimidating and oppressing others. All too often, only a serious blow to their pocketbooks, reputations, and psyches gets them to really look at their destructive ways and prods them to follow another route.

Clearly, not getting what you want at times is the very catalyst needed to develop spiritual qualities and values. But who goes around wishing for poverty, a disease, busted relationships, or a prison sentence to help change destructive behaviors? Precious few individuals! This is why I tell people before you ask for something, *surrender!* Then take the time to *align* yourself with Spirit and to understand what Spirit really wants for you. Consider if what you are asking for will *contribute* to the well-being of other people and not just yourself.

> ***When you seek to attract something,***
> ***remember to surrender,***
> ***align, and contribute!***

Of course, for most people it is easy to start out focusing mainly on yourself. For example, think of five things you would really like to have right now. I'll give you my quick list: a new home, a Mercedes, a new wardrobe, a loving partner, and continued good health. There, I've used up five wishes from the genie in the bottle. Let's just take a look at these for a moment.

From an ego standpoint everything on my list makes good sense. Who doesn't want a home to live in? Surely that request shouldn't be denied by Spirit. However, one reason I am currently motivated to write this book is because I don't have a residence and am sequestered at a friend's home, where I am massively focused on being productive because I have no other choice. Wait a minute! Does the fact that I don't have my own home during this transitional time help me to be more productive and of service to a higher purpose that I am only beginning to understand at this moment?

What about the Mercedes? Now, I already have a really reliable car. It even gets good gas mileage and is good for the environment. Though a Mercedes would be my car of choice, how do I really know if I am meant to have this vehicle? Do I just demand it of Spirit, or wait and see if Spirit really wants this car for me? The same could be said of the new wardrobe, the loving partner, and even continued good health. You see, if you step out of your ego and embrace uncertainty, you may not know what is best. You may not see clearly the larger picture Spirit is painting for your life. Now, I'm as human as the next person. It's difficult to stop my desire body from wanting what it wants. That's why it helps to constantly align with Spirit, so your thoughts, feelings, and actions reflect spiritual values and loving soul inclinations.

Do your best to align
your thoughts, feelings, and actions
along the path of service.

The simplest way to align your thoughts is to model them after spiritual teachers who inspire you. The whole "What would Jesus do?" or "What would Buddha do?" movement is an example. Of course, I know some people who would like to know what Donald Trump would do and forget about everyone else! True, you don't have to pick only great spiritual teachers as role models. Doctors, lawyers, bankers, parents, teachers, and many others may inspire you. Just be sure that your role models really embrace ethical and spiritual values and behaviors. Then attempt to align your thoughts with what you believe theirs may be.

As for aligning emotions, all feelings simply indicate to you a certain need trying to get fulfilled. It is how you act upon them or emote them that can lead to something better or worse. The same is true of how you use your emotions with the law of attraction. Emotions are the power factor of the law of attraction. They give you the power, desire, motion, or motivation to get what you want or not.

However, emotions are frequently very hard to align with Spirit. They can act like a horse or a race car, ready and willing to get you to the goal fast, even if they run out of control and put you in danger in the process. Sometimes emotions act like car brakes, constantly stopping you from moving forward even when you know you should. In my work with clients, I emphasize the importance of keeping emotions in a healthy state. In this way, they don't block Spirit by being either too reckless or too sluggish in their expression. Emotions are also related to desire, so even more than with our thoughts, it is important to qualify these desires with a willingness to only want what Spirit wants.

Then there is the process of aligning your actions. It's one thing to think a positive thought or get yourself into a state of feeling positive and energetic. It's a whole other ball game to actually change your behaviors! Insight and enthusiasm help, but they are not enough. To use a well-known saying, "talk doesn't cook the rice." That's why aligning your actions by taking steps every day, even if they are small ones, to shape a positive direction is essential.

REMEMBERING *YOU* THROUGHOUT THE DAY

One of the best exercises you can practice on a daily basis to help you stay aligned with Spirit is remembering your big "you"—your spiritual self—throughout the day. Below are some ways to do this based on the Muslim practice of remembering to pray five times a day.

Dawn Prayer. As the sun rises, you move from sleep to waking consciousness. At the same time you shift from your natural identity as big "you" (or Spirit), achieved effortlessly during deep dreamless sleep, to little "you" (or ego). If you can remember to do so, affirm to yourself as you wake up your essential identity as Spirit and dedicate yourself to keeping connected to what Spirit wants from you throughout the entire day.

Noon Prayer. Around noontime take a moment for prayer. You can use a prayer from your spiritual tradition, a verse from scripture, or an affirmation. And, you can ask yourself, "How am I doing? Am I living this day as my ego, or as Spirit? Have I forgotten who I really am? If so, how can I realign as my highest and best self?"

Afternoon Prayer. Around 5:00 p.m. see if you have gone out of alignment with Spirit. If so, mentally create a soul story out of any difficult event that took place during the day. Emotionally, attempt to move into a more positive state. Physically, exercise, rest, eat well, or do something to help your body heal. Remember to reassert your essential identity as Spirit, allowing the love of the soul to guide you.

Evening Prayer. The sun has set. Take time to notice how often you handled the daily events as big "you" or as little "you." If you went out of alignment in any area, visualize yourself mentally, emotionally, and physically acting as Spirit would have liked you to act. Meditate or go into prayer for guidance to discover if you missed anything that Spirit was attempting to convey to you throughout the day.

Night Prayer. As you go to sleep, let the cares of the day drop away. Now is a time to remember one thing only—you are Spirit. Once again dissolve into the natural state of who you really are. Surrender to Spirit as you go to sleep. If need be, chant a word, phrase, affirmation, or piece of scripture silently to yourself as you drift away. Let Spirit help you let go of the little "you" so you can be who you really are as big "you" once more.

WHOM DOES IT SERVE?

How do you align your actions? One way is to stay focused on service. There is a great movie called *Excalibur* about the King Arthur saga and the quest for the Holy Grail. For some time, Arthur was a great and wise king. Then his wife had an adulterous affair with his best friend. Heartbroken, King Arthur neglected his duties as a king, and the land fell into despair and disarray. Searching for a way to bring the spirit of their king back to life, the Knights of the Round

Table set out to search for the Holy Grail, the magical cup that Jesus was said to have used at the Last Supper. At last, one knight, Perceval, found the Grail and was asked the following questions: "What is the Grail? Whom does it serve?" Though the answers in the movie are cryptic, essentially Perceval reminded King Arthur that no matter what had befallen him in life, he was still here on Earth to love and serve others. King Arthur moved out of his state of despair, forgave his wife and best friend, and took up his role as king again, remembering his obligation to be of service whether he felt like it or not.

This story is a metaphor for how the soul seeks to keep you on track, especially regarding your capacity to love. In *The Secret,* the claim is made that "love is the greatest emotion." I couldn't disagree more. As I see it, love is not an emotion at all. Love is a choice! Since love comes from the level of the soul and is often reflected in the emotions, that is where most people recognize it. I tell many of my clients, however, that love is like the ocean, and emotions are like the waves. Love is a constant in this world. Despite what you may believe, it is never in a state of flux. The more you can train yourself to dive under the waves and tap into the love of the soul, the more you will experience love at all times. And you will no longer be caught up in the emotional experience of love, which comes and goes like waves do.

Attempt to attract more love,
so you have the power to contribute to others.

SPIRIT SPARK
The Holy Grail

Unlike the law of attraction, the Holy Grail can only be used in service and for spiritual purposes. You can go on your own Holy Grail quest in your mind. Using your imagination, take yourself to a place you believe to be very sacred. It can be a church, mosque, synagogue, or a spot in nature. There you are going to communicate with your soul or a spiritual teacher you hold in high regard. Now, imagine this spiritual source offering you the Holy Grail to use in service in your life. What will this service activity look like? Give yourself time to really answer these questions in meditation. Be sure to note down any insights that emerge.

SERVE WHAT YOU ATTRACT

Yes, since emotions ebb and flow, sometimes you won't feel like loving someone else—or yourself for that matter. And, if you don't have a deep spiritual practice or have truly loving people around you, you may not even know how to love. That's understandable since I believe that most movies, books, television programs, and music speak about love, when it isn't love in the slightest. Addiction, neediness, lust, desire, heartbreak, codependency, jealousy, possessiveness, and other emotional states are what most people are conditioned to believe love is. Frankly, they're not. As you learn to get below the waves, you learn what love is really all about. Only then do your emotions and desires accurately reflect what love is. Only then will you get busy and let the Holy Grail act as a reminder that you are here to serve and contribute something of value in this world, whether it "feels good" or not. That's why the following injunction is also very valuable.

Desire to attract only
that which you can
lovingly be a good custodian of.

In our throwaway society, this is a lesson we especially need to learn. While millions of people lack on this planet, millions have an excess of stuff that they don't take care of in the least. Be it their bodies and creative capacities, or their children, parents, coworkers, employees, bank accounts, schools, parks, streets, homes, and multiple belongings—too much is being consumed, discarded, and even outright neglected and abused. By learning to surrender, align, and contribute—instead of ask, believe, and receive—as you use the law of attraction, you not only help your own life, but also the lives of humanity as a whole, since you are slowing down this destructive pattern.

Unfortunately, people frequently don't get to this point until they are emotionally saturated with getting what they want and feel empty and shallow compared to having cultivated spiritual values. But those who are wise have learned to balance things out. Like the equal-armed cross of the double dorje, they treat themselves, others, and all of their belongings well. And, in appreciating deeply whatever they have, their desires slow down, perhaps even leading them to live much simpler lifestyles compared to the storehouse of inner spiritual wealth they now possess.

SPIRIT STORY
Radical Realignment

Tammy wasn't your average teenager. She grew up on the streets of Los Angeles, where at a young age she was enticed into a neighborhood gang. After an incident in which she stabbed another young girl in a fight, Tammy went to juvenile hall. Once she had maintained a certain level of good behavior, she entered a home for troubled girls. In the 'hood, Tammy had close ties to her gang members. It seemed like they cared about her when no one else did. But

Tammy had never considered how that caring was leading her into a path of drugs and crime. While at the group home, Tammy discovered spirituality for the first time, and she realized that she could still find caring people while learning to lead a different kind of life. Her four years in that home were not always easy. She once joked that she probably made more money selling drugs on a really good day than most counselors made there in a month! Tammy may have been right, but soon she discovered that the counselors had something she didn't possess: peace of mind and the capacity to feel good about themselves. So Tammy readjusted her attitude. She even managed to find a way to put herself through college! Today, she is a social worker, happy to help youth learn that the love of self and the love of the soul can help you discover real love—the kind of love that won't lead you down a dark road; it will liberate you by opening up a life of faith and hope.

TAKE TIME TO ALIGN
Key Insights

1. When you seek to attract something, remember to surrender, align, and contribute!

2. Do your best to align your thoughts, feelings, and actions along the path of service.

3. Attempt to attract more love, so you have the power to contribute to others.

4. Desire to attract only that which you can lovingly be a good custodian of.

Chapter 6

Step 5
Watch and Listen

Your mind has two functions: to be still and to create. The creative element of the mind comes about when the thinking process is engaged for the sake of manifesting something the mind believes it wants or needs. People who are focused in their egos think primarily about what they are wanting to acquire next. Their minds are rarely still, and they rarely hear or see what the soul is attempting to communicate to them. You see, just as the soul is the bridge between Spirit and the ego, the mind is the bridge between the ego and the soul. Only as the mind becomes still can it access the soul and hear beyond its own selfish needs.

Train your mind to enter into silence
so it can hear the soul.

THE VALUE OF MEDITATION

Unfortunately, too many people have minds that are chaotic and undisciplined. Instead of thinking things through, they tend to act on emotional impulse. This is also known as "desire-mind." The mind is like a hungry animal, always craving experiences to keep itself happy and entertained. It lacks patience and rarely knows how to attract something of real value. It almost never stops to consider what Spirit wants it to have. It may even resort to manipulating and cheating others in order to attract what it wants.

How do you overcome desire-mind or find a way to use the mind to enter into silence so it can hear the soul? One of the best ways is through the process of meditation. In the Christian Bible there is a saying, "Be still and know God." By silencing the mind, you teach it to listen to something beyond its conditioned ways of thinking and its egotistical desires. You teach it to be sensitive and receptive to what the soul is attempting to communicate. But it can rarely communicate clearly unless the ego wants to listen. In *The Secret* they tell you like attracts like. They tell you thoughts are magnetic and have a frequency. This is entirely correct, which is why you must strive to live in higher, or soul, consciousness first. If you don't you will only attract the thoughts and magnetic frequency of your ego.

How do you become receptive to the magnetic frequency of soul thoughts? The best way is through meditation. There are many types of meditation practice. All are valuable. However, for the purpose of really listening to what the soul wants from you, the best type of meditation practice is *contemplative meditation.* Here the mind reaches a state of inner quiet, where thoughts barely arise or don't even surface at all. The mind is silent, yet, paradoxically, it is also totally awake and alert. It enters a state of almost hyperalert listening within the silence it enters into.

While attempting to enter this contemplative silence, it is common for beginners to nearly fall asleep or to go to sleep altogether. In a way they are "spacing out." I remember doing this in my first attempts. I felt as if I had gone to sleep, and yet I knew this had not happened. My mind went "somewhere," but I had no idea where. To me, it seemed similar to being in a trancelike hypnotic state. Though hypnotic trances have some value, they are not the goal of contemplative meditation where you are attempting to hear "the voice of the silence." And that "silent" voice of the soul communicates more frequently to you in a gentle whisper, rather than in a loud dramatic way, so it can nudge you in the right direction in your life.

Desire to infuse your ego with soul thoughts.

SPIRIT SPARK
Benefits of Meditation

Why is meditation so helpful? Here are just a few reasons. Meditation . . .

- quiets the nervous system, producing a greater level of physical health, youth, and vitality;

- brings about emotional tranquility, inner peace, stability, and joy;

- develops detachment, discernment, and a mindfulness, allowing you to perceive reality more clearly and to act in a more thoughtful manner;

- produces greater coordination between your thoughts, feelings, and actions, allowing you to achieve your goals with greater skill;

- helps you align your ego with the soul;

- expands your consciousness;

- inclines you toward living and loving in a more soulful and spiritual way; stimulates creativity, insight, and intuition.

CONTEMPLATIVE MEDITATION

There are all kinds of meditation practices. Contemplative meditation is perhaps one of the more formal types. The word *contemplate* implies turning one's mind into a "template" so it can become a quiet, awake, receptive, and intuitive instrument of your higher spiritual self. People who master this form of meditation experience not only mental stillness, but an inner awareness of light. Deep states of inner peace are also common. This can be an involved and difficult practice, but the basic steps are as follows.

1. **Physical Body.** Sit in a cross-legged position or in a chair in such a way that your body is comfortable and supported but not likely to cramp up or go to sleep. Take time to relax the muscles in your body, including the muscles in your jaw, around your eyes, and on your forehead. If need be, breathe calmly and quietly for a few minutes. Once your body is no longer a distraction, shift your attention away from it.

2. **Emotional Body.** Now focus on calming your emotions, both positive and negative. One way to accomplish this is through deep breathing to calm your nervous system and center yourself. You can also visualize your emotions becoming tranquil. A good way to do this is by seeing your emotions as a body of water that eventually becomes as still as glass. Once you experience your emotions as peaceful and at rest, drop your focus from them.

3. **Mental Body.** Here you become aware of the mental chatter of your thoughts. There are many methods to quiet the "monkey mind," as this mental chatter is often referred to as. Deep breathing and focusing your

attention on a word or series of words by chanting them out loud or silently to yourself are two excellent methods. My favorite, however, is to set the intent to enter into a state of quiet, receptive listening. Simply act is if there is something you very much want to hear from Spirit or your soul. Then, keep mentally quiet so you can listen to the response.

4. **Spiritual Body.** Once at this level, it is common for some people to feel as if they have rested their attention within the center of their heads. If need be, you can also imagine that your body-mind is a temple (the word *contemplation* includes the word *temple* within it) and that Spirit is filling up that temple with light, love, and spiritual power. Make sure to stay within a silent, contemplative space for five to ten minutes before coming out of it. As you do, your mind will often be stimulated with ideas, intuitions, and insights.

SILENCE FEEDS THE SOUL

Taking time to hear that still small voice can be difficult, especially if your life is too heavily immersed in the sights and sounds of this world. It is a sad fact that more than ever we live on a planet saturated with noise coming from television, radio, movies, the Internet, conversations with other people, the daily sounds of freeways, trains, airplanes, and so forth. Silence, it appears, has become a rare commodity. Yet it is primarily in silence that your soul is most able to get your attention. That's why meditation is so essential. Yes, even I admit that getting into a state of total silence isn't always easy. I am no longer able, as I was in my twenties and thirties, to live the same kind of secluded lifestyle.

Since my mid-thirties I have been absorbed in raising a child and making a living. I know how this lifestyle can make escaping from the world and shutting out external sounds difficult. At times I want to avoid meditation because my mind and body have become so fatigued. Thankfully, I know that without meditation, my nerves will only get that much more frazzled and my capacity to stay connected to my soul will diminish. So, even when I want to skip it, I am still inclined to practice. I am also aware of the many other benefits meditation bestows. When you reach a deep state of meditation, it is very similar to entering a deep state of sleep. In deep dreamless sleep the body is better able to fully rejuvenate itself. Numerous times, I have started a meditation practice agitated and tired, yet I have come out of it feeling refreshed and at peace.

As the mind is silenced and opens to the soul, insights for resolving the difficulties you encounter in life frequently occur. Just remember that the answers don't always come immediately during a meditation. It isn't that the soul is unwilling to talk to you when you need it to. It's that the mind doesn't always hear or understand what the soul is trying to say. Just as you may recall something when you no longer zeroed in on trying to remember it, the mind often hears the soul only when it drops its tight focus on getting a solution right here and now. Thus, answers often come some time after a meditation, when the mind is preoccupied with other things.

Use meditation and other intuitive
practices to pay attention to
what the soul is trying to communicate.

Intuitive Aids

During meditation, the soul tends to communicate to the ego through a symbolic language. This isn't because the soul is intentionally trying to be vague and mysterious. The soul has a language of its own and until the ego becomes more aware of how that language operates, the ego only sees glimpses or hears bits and pieces of what the soul is trying to convey. In addition to meditation there are other tools you can use to access this symbolic language of the soul. Many of these tools have now entered mainstream consciousness, and more and more people are practicing them. But they can only be used to effectively access the soul if the ego is intent upon being receptive to what the soul has to say. Otherwise, the means I am about to share are reduced to fortune-telling, entertainment, and mere curiosity.

Dream Interpretation. During sleep, your mind goes through a process of shutting down. At first, your mind will be preoccupied with thoughts of the day. Then it will enter the rapid eye movement (REM) stage when dreams are most likely to take place. As it continues to shut down, it will enter the same state as found in contemplative meditation, only it will do this in an unconscious manner. This is when you enter deep dreamless sleep, the place where the ego is most likely to dissolve back into its natural oneness with Spirit. As you wake up, your mind goes through a reverse process, moving from deep dreamless sleep, to the dream stage, to becoming awake and thinking about the day. This explains why people typically remember glimpses of dreams just as they are waking up.

Learning to remember and understand dreams is an art. In my life, I have been fortunate to have had some training with noted dream interpreter Jeremy Taylor. Jeremy goes beyond simply creating an extensive list of symbols and their common meanings you can apply to your dreams. His "Ten Basic Hints for Dreamwork," found in his book, *The Living Labyrinth: Exploring Universal Themes in Myths, Dreams, and the Symbolism of Waking Life,* help guide you into deeper levels of dream interpretation. Of the ten hints that Jeremy gives, one of my favorites is how "only the dreamer can say with any certainty what meanings his or her dream may hold." If an interpretation really feels right, you will tend to have an "Aha!" experience around it. It just sounds or feels correct. Jeremy also advises on how dreams frequently have a layer of meaning and how "no dream comes just to tell the dreamer what he or she already knows." All ten tips are really helpful. You might also want to check out Jeremy's *Dream Work* for guidance on how to recall, record, and interpret your dreams.

Symbolic Cards. There are a variety of ways you can access your intuition through symbolic cards. When I was a girl, I had a box of Bible verses by my bed; I would simply draw a card when I needed guidance to assist me. I have also used tarot decks, rune stones, the *I Ching,* medicine wheel cards, Inner Child cards, and a variety of inspirational decks to get a symbolic sense of how I might break through, clarify, or gain insight into a problem in my life. I also keep a copy of the Christian Bible so I can access verses as needed. I have a notepad and pen available so I can write down any insights that come before I go to bed and after I wake up in the morning. I use this notepad to help me interpret dreams when I wake up as well.

Just be sure when you use any symbolic system that you understand it is only a symbol. Avoid slipping into fortune-telling. You are not using the cards to psychically predict the future, but to stay open to your own intuition so you can better hear what the soul may be attempting to communicate. Also, learn to combine any use of symbolic cards with common sense. Let both your left brain (the logical part) and your right brain (the intuitive part) guide your understanding.

DIVINE COINCIDENCES

Synchronicities. Like dreams and symbols, synchronicities can indicate soul attempts to communicate to the ego. Synchronicities are events that appear to be coincidental but are not. They may be a result of a telepathic interchange taking place between two people, like when you think about someone and then that person suddenly calls you. They may also be a result of thoughts and feelings using the law of attraction to manifest a particular intent, like that parking space opening up for you after you set the intent that it be there as your car arrives.

Though they are interesting, these types of synchronicities do not necessarily involve the soul. Remember, the soul only cares about your capacity to be of service. If you "accidentally" missed getting out the door on time and then just happened to be there for a call from a friend in need, then your soul may have been involved. But, more frequently, soul synchronicities involve the soul attracting to your ego opportunities that can help move it along the right path. This is more commonly known as "luck."

There is a popular saying attributed to General George Patton that luck is really preparation meeting opportunity. Especially when we are prepared by regularly aligning our egos with the soul and listening to what it wants from us in meditation, we attract opportunities to be of service into our lives. And, if we are not prepared, then our egos will not be able to handle effectively the good opportunities that the soul is attempting to attract our way. We will miss out on that great job, perfect partner, or chance to say or do the right thing.

This is also known as a poor sense of timing. Your ego is out of alignment with your soul, causing you to act in an impulsive way mentally, emotionally, or even physically. Review your life for a moment. Have you ever jumped too quickly and ended up with a relationship, job, business, or other opportunity that was only partly what you were really hoping for? Or, did something or someone appear that was everything you wanted but you were too impulsive to take the time to wait for the person or opportunity to respond to you in the right way? In both of these cases, you might have thought and even felt right, but you were too impatient to make sure the timing was right! When synchronicities happen, especially when they come from the soul, they are like doors of opportunity opening up and inviting you to take a leap. Just be sure you are prepared for that opportunity in the right way, so you can better ensure that you will jump through the right door!

> *Only as the mind learns the disciplines*
> *of meditation and develops intuition can it use*
> *the law of attraction in the correct way.*

SPIRIT STORY
Prayer Warrior

Karen never intended to be a single mother of four. But then her husband of eleven years walked out, leaving her in shock and a great deal of fear. Though Karen was overwhelmed for a time, the strength of her spiritual practice and faith helped her through. At first she was ashamed to reach out to other people, but eventually she knew she had to in order to help her family survive. She was not aware of meditation, but she was inclined toward prayer. So she went to her local church and found a group of "prayer warriors" who would pray for each other on a daily basis. Through prayer, Karen learned to receive guidance, and with that guidance she realized how strong she could be. And she knew that she was loved despite the difficult circumstances in which she found herself. As the years went by, Karen continued her regular practice of prayer. She also kept up her association with some sort of prayer group. To her amazement, she eventually found a good job as a loan officer, purchased a home for her family, and even sent two of her children to college. Finally, with her youngest now a teenager, Karen has even opened up to love again and is dating a man she enjoys. What is Karen's secret to success? Never forget who you really are! Don't let anyone take that from you, no matter how difficult life gets. Believe in yourself, find a way to communicate with Spirit, and things will work out for the better in the end.

WATCH AND LISTEN
Key Insights

1. Train your mind to enter into silence so it can hear the soul.

2. Desire to infuse your ego with soul thoughts.

3. Use meditation and other intuitive practices to pay attention to what the soul is trying to communicate.

4. Only as the mind learns the disciplines of meditation and develops intuition can it use the law of attraction in the correct way.

Chapter 7

Step 6
Order Your Thoughts

Our thoughts are creative. We already know that long before there were telephones, televisions, microwaves, automobiles, books, movies, and cell phones, they were all thoughts in someone's mind. Everything begins with an idea, then a plan to bring that idea to fruition, and then the impetus and effort to make it so. Just as humans create, Spirit creates. The universe, planets, animals, humans, and all of nature began in the "mind of God." As *The Secret* states, "Your current thoughts are creating your life. What you think about the most will appear as your life." All I can say is, "Yes and no!" Why is this so? Simple:

> *Your thoughts do not create everything*
> *that happens in your life.*
> *We do not live in an isolated world.*

Your Mind and Their Mind

As I have illustrated in this book, Spirit and the soul think as well. When you are born, you enter into a world already full of thought.

Our planet was thought into existence by God. And the planet, which is a living being, also has a mind of its own. Just as you have the cells of your body living within you attempting to understand what you are thinking about, we live as "cells" within the planet and benefit from trying to understand where our planet wants us to go.

Then there are the ancient thoughts of other human beings—their philosophies, cultures, and beliefs. These explain why, when you travel around the globe, people can seem so different. Even in our modern era, there are people who live and think much as their ancestors did thousands of years ago.

Groups of people also think along certain lines, creating what has been called at times "group think" or "group mind"! Their thoughts impact one another for better or for worse. This shouldn't surprise you.

*There is such a thing as
"group mind" or "group think."
Others can impact your thinking
for better or worse.*

SPIRIT SPARK
Group Mind

So, you want to finally manifest that beach house? Well, here are just a few others who might be thinking about it too:

1. Spirit. Which may have other plans in mind for you.

2. Other Prospective Buyers. Who may be trying to manifest the same home you want for themselves.

3. Family and Friends. Including your partner, parents, siblings, and others who may be jealous of your beach house, feel you are not ready to be responsible for one, or may not want you to live there for other reasons.

4. The Government. Which wants to use that beach house land for some other purpose.

5. And more! Put your own ideal of previously unknown and unseen thoughts here.

Finally, within this mix of thought all around you, your own thoughts exist. Though in a sense thoughts create your life, they do so mainly according to the way you interpret, or give meaning, to events. These events may not always have been thought up by you. They may have been thought up by Spirit, your soul, the planet, or other human beings around you who have put certain circumstances into motion. It is even possible that people who were completely innocent and did not have negative thoughts (or "vibrate" at a negative "frequency" as *The Secret* describes it) have simply gotten caught in the crosshairs of what have turned into negative events. They may have been simply innocent, naive, or attempting to be of service when they wound up in hurtful, dangerous, and harmful situations.

SOUL STORIES AND EGO STORIES

Applied to the law of attraction, the best you can do is learn how to make meaning, or create what I call a soul story, out of any negative events that occur. These soul stories in turn set up the probability that you will attract an abundance of spiritual wisdom, which will help you respond to other similar events with the spiritual power you need to handle them well. Soul stories give you greater clarity, compassion, love, and understanding regarding the events that have taken place in your life. To put it simply, you learn from your mistakes and lessen the odds that they will happen again. In this way soul stories help you create a more positive future. They keep you connected with Spirit, allowing you to be more creative because you are likely to perceive situations clearly, helping you to be a more effective attractor.

Now not everyone makes up soul stories. Often they make up what I call ego stories instead, which tend to emphasize primarily the negative. Or else they personalize events and feed the ego's need to play the See Me game. The situations become all about you, and this distorts your capacity to think about and perceive events clearly. They stir up your emotions, filling you with confusion, fear, hatred, envy, arrogance, self-pity, and negativity. Ironically, the notion that you create everything that happens in the universe can also become an ego story. From a metaphysical perspective, yes, we are all one. If I am one with Spirit, then, *as* Spirit, "I" created everything that has ever happened in this universe, including all the good and all the bad. However, Spirit manifests in billions of people on this planet alone. So even though "I" (Spirit) created everything, to think that "I" (Lisa Love) created it all is absurd and a hugely egotistical statement.

Can I create soul stories that are filled with insight and compassion and help influence the overall trend of group thought toward greater good? Yes! Will any ego stories that focus on "what's in it for me" only increase the suffering and negativity in the world? Yes! Which is why with any event you are presented with a choice: Which story (soul or ego) will you choose? Of course that choice depends upon a number of factors. How aligned with the soul are you? How influential is your ego? How capable are you of thinking and perceiving in a clear and conscious—or in a muddled and confused—way? And, how chaotic or clear is your emotional state?

These factors all make up whatever story (or the overall dominant thought process, as *The Secret* calls it) you tell about yourself and your life. So decide now. Will your stories be from the level of your ego, which will lead to more chaos, hurt, and suffering? Or will they be from the level of your soul, taking you to a place of greater understanding, peace, and joy?

Remember some events just happen
and may not be your fault.
It is the story you tell yourself about events,
not the events themselves, that counts.

CREATING A SOUL STORY

A soul story turns any event that happens in your life into an opportunity for spiritual growth. No matter how painful or traumatic, any event can help you develop the soul qualities of compassion, forgiveness, and wisdom. (A more extensive list of qualities can be found in chapter 3, Engage the Soul.) A recent example of an attempt to create a soul story takes place in the movie *Pan's Labyrinth*. Living with a brutal stepfather, a young girl struggles to maintain her spiritual integrity through the use of story. The basic elements for creating a soul story are as follows:

1. **Name the Event.** Soul stories are not naive. They do not deny the reality of a situation. To fully mature spiritually after an event, you must own what occurred.

2. **Identify a Soul Quality.** Find one or more specific soul qualities you are being called to cultivate because of the event.

3. **Allow the Soul to Heal You.** Let the love, wisdom, discernment, compassion, joy, courage, or other soul qualities help you heal whatever pain or trauma you may be suffering from.

4. **Cultivate the Soul Quality.** As you heal, work to embody more of the soul quality you are meant to learn about.

5. **Expand Your Soul.** Remember, you are not alone in your struggle or difficulty. Avoid making your trauma all about you. Open your eyes and see who else needs love, support, and friendship to recover from a wound similar to yours.

6. **Engage in Soul Karma.** Next turn your "bad" karma into soul, or "service," karma by teaching others what you have learned from the experience so they are better able to cope with similar painful circumstances in their own lives.

7. **Pray for the Soul in Others.** Realize that anyone who has harmed you does so due to a lack within themselves. Though you cannot control whether they will develop soul qualities for themselves, you can send positive thoughts their way that they may one day do so.

8. **Share Your Soul Story.** Once you are healed, share your story so others can benefit from the lessons and soul qualities the event has helped you learn.

At last we come to a very important spot in this book. From this point forward the use of the law of attraction splits into two directions. Prior to these words the steps I have given to you can only be used by those who seek to apply the law of attraction in a spiritual way, helping them to be an agent for light, love, and spiritual power in the world. Now all the techniques and information I will be sharing can be used from either the level of the soul or the level of the ego. Again, the ego has three aspects: mind, feelings, and body. The mind is filled with thoughts, and those thoughts are creative. Ideally before that mind creates it will orient toward Spirit, negate the ego, engage the soul, align the three aspects of the ego with the soul, and seek through meditation and the cultivation of the intuition to attract spiritual abundance before seeking material abundance. Or, it will not! Hoping you are by this point absolutely clear about this, let's proceed with learning the primary techniques of how to order your thoughts and be creative with your mind to attract and manifest something in the world from either spiritual or egotistical motivation.

Visualization. Everyone possesses the capacity to imagine things. For people with a highly developed visual sense, seeing pictures while they imagine is easy. As applied to the law of attraction, visualization helps the mind shape impressions and ideas into something less abstract and more concrete. Visualization is also used to program the emotions and body to act along certain lines. You simply imagine with as much detail as you can what you hope to attract, reinforce your desire to attract it, and through this process enhance your ability to receive it or carry it out.

Some people, like me, are not particularly visual. They tend to have other senses developed. I am mainly auditory. I hear thoughts more than see images. This doesn't mean you can't visualize. You may just have to train yourself to do so. I started by visualizing simple images with my eyes closed—like a star, a triangle, the sun, and so forth. Eventually, you can add in more detail. In fact, the more detail the better! You can even make your visualization a multisensory experience. *The Secret* tells you to imagine yourself in a car—feeling your hands on the wheel and the texture of the fabric on your body, hearing the hum of the car, and sensing your excitement as you drive down the road.

The more you visualize something the more real it seems. And the more it stirs up the emotional desire to attract it into your life. If you visualize getting a new Mercedes on a regular basis, you are likely to put your energy into actually owning it. That's because energy follows thought. If that thought is spiritually motivated, what you attract will not have a negative impact on your life. You will be able to appreciate what you have and treat it well. It will bring pleasure to your life, but you will not be attached to it. If that thought is egotistically motivated, what you attract will cause problems down the road. Maybe you won't be able to afford the Mercedes payments. Maybe you risk taking the money to buy the Mercedes out of your children's college funds, diminishing their chances for success to enhance only yourself. Maybe you only want that Mercedes as a status symbol to play the See Me game to impress others and cover up your own low sense of self-worth. The end result will be the same. You will have the car of your dreams (or visualization), but it will not keep you happy for long. So back you will go to the ego's perpetual nightmare of wanting more and more and more!

Affirmations. An affirmation is a word or a series of words that you repeat over and over again either out loud or in your mind. Because of their repetitious nature, affirmations start to shape your beliefs. The more you believe in an affirmation, the more likely it is to shape your thoughts, feelings, and behavior.

Affirmations are not necessarily spiritual in nature. Consider what would happen if you repeated this series of words over and over again: "No matter what it takes, I'm going to get my revenge on that person." Chances are you would head down a path that wasn't too good for you or the other individual! That is why it is important to select positive affirmations that help you develop your spiritual nature and increase your odds of being a joyful and loving person.

Depending on the strength of your belief and the potency of your desire, affirmations will, or will not, work. For example, if you say out loud, "I am my perfect weight" and then think sarcastically, "Yeah, right," your affirmation won't work very well. That is why many law of attraction teachers talk about getting your feelings into agreement with your thoughts to help your affirmations manifest.

Also, when you create your affirmations, be careful that they are not egotistical in nature. Ego affirmations tend to be absolute and focus on getting something specific like money, a new car, a partner, a job promotion, etc. Soul affirmations emphasize developing spiritual qualities instead. They help you cultivate the skills you need to not only attract but maintain in a spiritual way what you acquire.

Soul versus Ego Affirmation Examples

Ego: "I am with the ultimate partner of my dreams."
Soul: "Each and every day I will become a more loving partner so I am worthy of attracting a loving partner in return."

Ego: "I will win the race."
Soul: "I will put forth my best effort, maximizing all my skills, so I increase the likelihood that I will win the race."

Ego: "I am making 'x' amount of money by the end of this year."
Soul: "I will become a more effective steward of money, enabling me to attract more."

Ego: "My body is in a state of perfect health."
Soul: "More and more I learn about and live according to healthy habits so my body-mind lives as an increased reflection of health no matter what state it is in."

ORDERING YOUR THOUGHTS

Visualizations and affirmations are useful tools, but for many people they are too abstract and difficult to use. The following techniques help correct this by taking an image that is only in your head and getting it down on paper where you can see it every day. They can help you really sort out what it is that you are wanting and how to go about getting it.

Vision Boards. Vision boards are especially useful if you have trouble visualizing or if you want a constant physical reminder to help you focus on what you are trying to attract into your life. The basic technique is simple. Just get a bunch of magazines, photos, and word labels, and sort through them to find the things you hope to attract.

Some people will even tell you to map out your vision board according to feng shui principles of how to lay out a room, known as the bagua. There are nine sections to a bagua map. For example, you put items related to wealth and prosperity in the upper-left corner. Below this you put items related to health and family. Knowledge and self-cultivation go below that. In the top-center area, you put fame and reputation; items that represent the center of your being below that; and career goals and aspirations are placed at the bottom. Relationships you want to strengthen or hope to attract go in the upper-right corner. Children, creativity, or your playful inner child go below relationships. Helpful people and travel go to the lower-right quadrant.

If you want, you can even make a separate vision board for each one of these themes. Just be sure to keep any vision boards in an obvious place where you look at them often. If possible, spend time viewing the images, words, and photos on a daily basis. As you look at the board, you might even journal your thoughts, feelings, and an action plan regarding how well you are manifesting what you want. Prayer is also useful and keeps you oriented toward Spirit while you are looking at your board.

Mind Maps. Mind-mapping is a popular tool to help stimulate your creativity and focus your thoughts. There are even software programs available that assist you in this process. Typically, you begin with a central image or idea. For example, the central image could be a picture of yourself. Next, you create branches that shoot off from the center. As a law of attraction technique, you might put branches for relationships, money, career, spiritual practice, health, and so forth. Then, you create smaller branches off of these bigger ones. Let's say you want to focus on money. You could create a branch for your current financial situation, including your various debts and assets. Other branches could contain your investment, retirement, education, travel, housing, and other goals.

As you create your mind map, you can generate as many branches and subbranches as you want. You may even want to create more than one mind map. Money could become an entire mind map, or relationships, and so forth. On your map, you can put your various thoughts and feelings. Next to retirement, you might put the words, "feeling anxious." Or, you could draw a worried face. Any kind of image can be used. As you anticipate reaching a retirement goal, you could put a happy face or images of how you are living your life once you are finally retired. You can also add various colors and other features that speak to you.

In general, mind maps help you quickly see your goals, difficulties, and possibilities. They help you visualize, classify, organize, structure, and study your thoughts, feelings, and courses of action. And, they help you get a quick overview that aids you in problem-solving and decision-making.

The more you use any of these four techniques, the more proficient your mind will become with creative processing. Having said this, I leave you with one final warning.

When you do use your own mind to create events, be careful. You may get what you wish for. Be sure that your wish doesn't become a regret.

SPIRIT STORY
Renewing a Relationship

John was an average guy. He owned a flooring business and had been married for twenty-six years. He loved his wife, but felt a little bored with the relationship. Over time, it seemed they had lost the magic that had existed in their early years together. What John didn't realize was that he was feeding the notion that the relationship was boring with these thoughts and feelings. Hoping he could break out of the rut, he planned a trip to Europe, where he and his wife would celebrate their anniversary. Though that may have given them a spark, I encouraged John to do some deeper work that would help him reprogram his thoughts and emotions about his wife. I asked him to put together a one-hundred-page anniversary book. On each page, I instructed him to write a favorite memory of his wife or their time together. He could also put something he really appreciated about her. John's initial reaction was a huge sigh. That would be so much work! Would he even find one hundred things to write about? I encouraged him to try, and eventually he completed the book. I then told him to take the book to Europe and share it with his wife on the day of their anniversary, which he did. To John's amazement and great delight, his wife was so moved by the gift that they experienced what felt like a second honeymoon! Better yet, their relationship entered a greater level of joy and appreciation for each other, which continues to this day.

ORDER YOUR THOUGHTS
Key Insights

1. Your thoughts do not create everything that happens in your life. We do not live in an isolated world.

2. There is such a thing as "group mind" or "group think." Others can impact your thinking for better or worse.

3. Remember some events just happen and may not be your fault. It is the story you tell yourself about events, not the events themselves, that counts.

4. When you do use your own mind to create events, be careful. You may get what you wish for. Be sure that your wish doesn't become a regret.

Chapter 8

TWO Techniques

STEP 4

Take Time to Align

Starting with an attitude of surrender,
align the three aspects of your ego—
thoughts, feelings, and body—
with Spirit. Take time to make sure
each part is committed to
making a contribution.

Anytime you enter into a meditative state and begin to receive intuitions and insights, it is easy to get out of alignment. This is done in a number of ways. Mentally, you may start to dissect, analyze, and take apart your intuitions and insights too quickly. Emotionally, you may doubt what you have received, get anxious about what the insights mean, or be too enthusiastic and sporadic in your intention to manifest what has inspired you. Physically, you may not have the right amount of stamina or energy. You may also fail to get the resources you need to practically see the inspirations through. Or, your sense of timing may be off, making you too slow or quick to implement what you need.

Because of this, commitment is essential. Commitment begins when you possess an inner resolve to see something through even when difficulties or obstacles arise. The depth of your commitment is based upon the strength of your intent. Without this, you will let go of something you are attempting to manifest before it has a real chance to emerge. Of course, you don't want to make a commitment that is too absolute either. Why persist down a path that is too overwhelming for you to handle? Knowing how to generate and sustain the right amount of commitment to sufficiently, wisely, and reasonably see something through is an art. Doing all you can, without doing something that harms yourself or others in the process, is important.

It is difficult to be really committed to something or someone if you are not in alignment with it or fully behind it. This is the main reason numerous inspirations disappear into a vaporous mist. To stay aligned you need to continually orient toward Spirit. It doesn't matter that you don't fully understand how to make the idea happen. It is not even important that you feel completely great about what you are attempting. It is normal for emotions to fluctuate between enthusiasm and fear or excitement and anxiety. In time, you will learn to see more clearly on a mental level what is required to get the job done. After you weather a few emotional highs and lows in relation to what you are trying to manifest, your feelings will sort themselves out. This is why it can help to test the strength of a commitment by relying on your body, and not just your thoughts and feelings for support.

I learned how important it is to make decisions based upon how solid, or right, something feels in your body during my training in somatic (body) psychology. Some people call this a "gut feeling," but experience has taught me that it is really much more than that. If something is really right, it feels solid everywhere. It is almost as if the head, heart, stomach, arms, legs, and all parts of the body are saying, "Yep, this is it! We can support this. We can make it through this one." Call it stamina or resolve; I just know that if your body is in agreement, a commitment is easier to follow through on.

And with your body going along with the inspiration, your thoughts and feelings more rapidly come into alignment. This is because all experiences happen at a sensorial level first. We sense something before we interpret it mentally or express it emotionally. This sensation might be tingling, warming, electrifying, calming, energizing, or solidifying. Whatever it is, it will help indicate to you that surrender is warranted and commitment is possible.

SPIRIT SPARK
Breathe Deeply

Breathing is essential to your survival. And this happens to be true on a variety of levels. As you learn to breathe properly, you can relax your nervous system, calm your emotions, and clarify and bring stillness to your mind. Advanced breathing techniques also teach you how to bring more energy into your body, balance your male and female energies, and cultivate poise in your overall personality. An excellent resource to help you along these lines is *The Breathing Box* (book, CD, and DVD) by Gay Hendricks, PhD.

STEP 5
Watch and Listen

*After aligning the ego with Spirit, enter into
meditation. As you meditate, be attentive
and curious about discovering what Spirit
most wants you to attract into your life at this time.*

By this step you have already mastered the most difficult stages of the manifestation process. These stages have helped you to come from a motive of service to cultivating harmlessness. Remember, love always carries within it the seed of doing the least harm. Visualize your intent to be harmless as an offering to Spirit. Then begin the meditative process. As you get insights during the meditative process, write them down, or be sure to journal them right afterward. Remember, these insights may come some time after a meditative practice, so be ready to make note of them whenever they arise.

You can also take a piece of paper, like a 3-by-5-inch index card, and just as you go to bed write down a question on the card that you are very curious to receive an answer to. You might want to read the question several times over before setting the card down and going to sleep. Or, you can repeat the question to yourself a number of times as you drift off into your dream state.

Then, right as you wake up, pay attention to whatever images, thoughts, feelings, or dream memories immediately come into your mind. Write them down, if possible, on the back of the index card on which you posed your question. If the insights regarding your question are still unclear, ask for clarification the following night as you go to sleep. Eventually, the answers will come into greater focus.

As you do this exercise, remember to avoid waking up to loud sounds like an alarm or jarring music. If you need an alarm or music to help you get up at a certain time, make sure the sound is at least gentle in nature so your early morning intuitive responses are not disturbed. Also be sure to give yourself extra time in the morning to do this exercise. Set your alarm fifteen to thirty minutes earlier than you need to wake up if necessary.

SPIRIT SPARK
Quick Meditation Tips

Before you meditate, apply some of these basic guidelines.

1. If you are a beginning meditator, try not to meditate for more than twenty minutes at a time.

2. Make sure you are in a quiet environment where you will not be interrupted. And don't forget to turn off the phones and to silence ticking clocks!

3. Especially if you are just starting out, attempt to meditate around the same time and in the same place. This will help you establish the habit.

4. Though some forms of meditation can be done lying down, contemplative meditation works best if you sit up and keep the spine erect.

5. In general, people meditate with their eyes closed. To avoid eyestrain you may want to remove any contact lenses. If you do decide to keep your eyes open, fix them slightly downward on a spot that will not be too distracting.

6. As you enter into meditation, try to approach it with an attitude of love and reverence. Remember you are attempting to communicate with Spirit.

STEP 6

Order Your Thoughts

Create soul stories so you are more likely to receive various ideas, intuitions, and insights from Spirit. Then, order your thoughts so you can carry out the wishes of Spirit.

At last, we are at the stage of the manifestation process where thought kicks into full force. Now it is time to activate the mind and build a solid mental structure around what you are trying to create. It might surprise you that this step comes so far down the list of techniques because the majority of law of attraction books have you begin here. They encourage you to sit down and think about what you want. Then think about how to get it. As I have revealed in this book, it is a bit more complicated when you consider who is doing the thinking—your ego or the Spirit within you?

Though it may be impossible to be absolutely certain that your thoughts are coming entirely from a spiritual versus an egotistical level (odds are your desire is a mixture of both), at least by following the techniques I have outlined, you increase the odds that Spirit has a majority of say in the matter. And you are less likely to be driven by fear because you let Spirit guide the process more.

At this stage, your thoughts will no longer be general. Instead, they will be more specific and concrete as you begin to create the blueprint, or mental structure, about how to make your idea come true. Rather than saying simply, "I would like to start a business," you begin to mentally plan out your business strategy. You think more clearly about the type of business you want—its location, product, clientele, marketing strategy, employees, and so forth. The better thought out the blueprint, the more likely it will manifest without difficulty. Of course, if you think it through too much and don't leave room for creative surprises, synchronicities, and more marvelous inspirations and intuitions, you can run into a different kind of trouble because

Spirit always continues to inspire. If you get too fixed on your game plan, you cut off this natural flow from Spirit. John Lennon, one of the famous Beatles, was known to have said, "Life is what happens to you while you're busy making other plans." As you make your plans, be sure that life, or Spirit, still has a say in what is going on.

Keeping this in mind, start making your plans using tools like visualization, affirmations, vision boards, and mind maps to help you refine and see more clearly what you are trying to manifest. Or, if you are adept at thinking things through on your own without these aids, go right ahead. You might even want to enlist the help of coaches, consultants, mentors, and others who can give you direction. Remember, a humble mind that is oriented toward Spirit appreciates enlisting the wisdom and support of others who have previously traveled down the same path.

SPIRIT SPARK
Tune in to Your Mind

An excellent method for working with affirmations and visualizations is through the use of audio CDs. There are many CDs you can try, but I recommend those by Dr. Bernie Siegel, a pediatric surgeon and pioneer in the mind-body field. His *Meditations for Peace of Mind, Meditations for Morning and Evening,* and *Meditations for Enhancing Your Immune System* are my favorites. I also enjoy *101 Power Thoughts* by respected spiritual teacher Louise L. Hay. Some of these CDs are meant to be used as you go to bed or when you are able to close your eyes. Others can be used while driving in a car, taking a walk, or working out at the gym. Whatever CD you pick, it is essential that you use it often, usually for thirty days, and even as much as two to three times a day.

The THREE Stage

Manifesting What Spirit Wants

Now that you have a clear understanding of what you want to manifest, it is time to attract it into your life. These final steps help you do that.

STEP 7

Tap into Your Feelings

As you continue to respond to what Spirit wants for you, be aware of the various feelings that surface. By inquiring into the need of the emotion and changing your thinking, you vibrate your feelings to a higher level.

STEP 8

Highlight the Shadow in Others

Understand that as you implement what Spirit wants for you, others may not always react in a favorable way. Notice, or highlight, what the resistance in others may be, then cope with, transform, or walk away from it as needed.

STEP 9

Remove the Shadow from Yourself

Now, take time to understand the various ways you may be resisting what Spirit wants for you. If needed, ask others to assist you in removing the various blocks you may have to manifesting what Spirit wants.

STEP 10

Execute and Easy Does It!

Aligned with Spirit and committed to doing what Spirit wants, execute your plan to attract what is needed to be of service in some area of your life. And remember to let it flow! Keep Spirit involved in the process as you go.

Chapter 9

⚜

Step 7
Tap into Your Feelings

By far, the majority of law of attraction books focuses on this step, helping you work more effectively with your emotions. Emotions are thought to be "the power factor of manifestation." They are the seat of desire. If you generate enough emotional energy, you create the power to get what you want through the sheer force of your emotional will. Emotions simply feel, want, and express what they want—which is why they need to be directed by both the power of the mind and the power of your soul so they become refined. As you learn to calm your emotions, they can better see and absorb what Spirit is trying to convey.

BEFRIEND YOUR FEELINGS

Sadly, too many people have thoughts colored with emotion. And their emotional desires are colored with the needs and impulses of the ego so that they don't know how to be soulful. How do you overcome this? One of the best ways can be found in a number of psychological, spiritual, and law of attraction books. You need to understand what your feelings are trying to convey to you so you can gain emotional mastery over them. You do this by befriending any feeling and by consistently learning to vibrate your emotional responses to a more peaceful, loving, and soulful state.

Every feeling has a gift to give you,
and all feelings are your friends.

As I have said before, there are no good or bad feelings. There are only needs trying to get fulfilled. Here are some examples:

- Sorrow reflects the need to let go or to release something or someone who is no longer serving the current phase of your life.

- Anger reveals the need to establish clear and protective boundaries so you can maintain a sense of integrity and respect when interacting with others.

- Jealousy is based on the need to feel more secure and assured that you have your own value and place in the world.

- Fear reflects the need to be alert to possible dangers around you so you can attentively and skillfully navigate through them.

- Confusion is simply the need to enter into a meditative state so you can sort out your priorities, which helps you better see and accept the truth of any situation.

- Being overwhelmed is just the need for space so you can relax and let go of that which is no longer of real importance in your life.

- Happiness is the need to embrace a transitory pleasure to absorb it fully.

- Joy is the need to embrace and express more of your soul so you can find peace and meaning in the world no matter what is happening around you.

Looked at in this way, it becomes easier to understand why there are no good or bad feelings. Emotions are simply the way you act upon your feelings. Feelings are simply the way you interpret particular sensations. Sensations come from living in a body with five senses and a nervous system. The five senses and the nervous system help you know this world as it is. Feelings and emotions help you know this world as well. You simply need to become more skillful at catching any feeling at the sensorial level so you can understand it and work with it more constructively before you emote it! Naturally, when you don't have this skill, you end up rapidly emoting and do not have a clear understanding of what is going on or what you need out of the situation you are confronted with. How does all of this relate to the law of attraction? As you learn to work with emotions more skillfully, you more rapidly attract to yourself the ability to fulfill your true needs, which are soul needs.

Emotional mastery helps you attract what you need to fulfill soul needs, not ego needs.

SPIRIT SPARK
Seeing Your Emotional Body

Chances are that you know when you are angry, sad, happy, confused, or experiencing another transitory emotion. But what is the overall state of your emotional health? One way to find out is to use water images to get a sense of how you tend to be emotionally on a daily basis.

Are you mostly like a calm, crystal-clear lake? Energetic like a rushing river? Moody, with a lot of hidden emotion, like a dark swamp? Frozen over like an icy lake? Calm on the surface with bits of ice or an entire iceberg of unresolved issues still lurking about? In the process of catharsis, causing you to cry often like rain coming down? Heavy with emotion like a sponge that is full of water? Subject to eruptions of anger like lava coming out of a volcano? Fun and sparkly like a babbling brook? Difficult to understand and confused, resulting in a dense fog? Emotionally predictable like ocean waves rolling in and out? Maybe you are a combination of all of the above! Once you have intuited what your overall emotional state looks like, go a step further. Use visualization techniques to imagine the clouds clearing, the ice melting, the volcanic eruptions lessening, the swamp clearing, and so forth. As you do this, eventually you will sense that your emotional body is filled with a steady hum of power, or energy, while at the same time increasingly in a state of tranquility and calm.

The Ego and Emotion

How does the ego deal with emotions? Let's start with the example of sorrow and its gift of detachment. When you cannot let go of that which no longer serves you, you begin the process of attachment, obsession, possessiveness, and hoarding. Remember, the ego cannot accept the fact of death, especially the death of itself and its constant notion that it is the center of the universe. So when the ego feels sorrow, instead of welcoming it, feeling it, grieving through it, and letting it go, the ego insists on holding on so it doesn't have to feel the loss of someone or something. Perhaps it will find a way to hang on to a dead relationship by always living in the past or remaining obsessed with someone it can no longer have. Or, it will set out on a quest to live a life of excess (seven cars, one hundred pairs of shoes, six different relationships) so it doesn't have to experience or feel loss ever again. The ego may try to convince itself by saying something like, "Who cares about that car, that pair of shoes, or that person? I've got plenty more on the side!"

In a similar way, when you feel jealous, you have a choice. Do you let your ego convince you that you must be the only rich, powerful, and attractive person in the universe? Do you insist that others around you must be stopped from making their own contribution with their unique inner gifts or qualities? Do you start down a path of trying to cut out all of the competition around you so no one can make you feel insecure or take you away from your perceived exclusive place in the world? Or, do you honor the soul in everyone since you know that everyone is interconnected at the level of Spirit? Therefore, no one can take anything away from you because you are, in a real sense, everyone and everywhere!

If you don't learn to handle your emotions in this more spiritual way, you will handle them egotistically, which leads to increased insensitivity. This shuts down the natural sensitive responses that your feelings are here to reveal to you. As you become a more insensitive person, you will also become more callous and superficial until, eventually, you don't feel anything at all. That's why I avoid the notion of replacing "bad" emotions with "good" ones. I want you to understand and feel all of your emotions and to avoid the idea that there are some you should not have. Just as you wouldn't want to poke out your eyes or cut off your ears, you don't want to start labeling feelings such as jealousy or anger as something you shouldn't have. Embrace all of your feelings. Then go a step further and uncover the need the feeling is trying to reveal. This helps you fulfill it in a soulful, instead of an egotistical, way. And here is the fun of this approach, especially when it comes to the desire aspect of the emotional body:

*Remember, as a soul, you don't have
to possess something. You can simply feel
or imagine that you possess it. As you
will discover, the feeling alone
is often enough to satisfy you.*

PRAYERS FOR EMOTIONAL PEACE

Prayers have been around forever and are, in many ways, the precursor to affirmations. Here are a few of my favorite prayers that I use in a way similar to affirmations, especially when my emotions get all stirred up.

A Prayer for Serenity

God grant me the serenity to accept
the things I cannot change,
the courage to change the things I can,
and the wisdom to know the difference.
—author unknown

A Prayer to Stay Spiritually Aligned

Lord, make me an instrument of thy peace.
Where there is hatred, let me sow love;
Where there is injury, pardon;
Where there is doubt, faith;
Where there is despair, hope;
Where there is darkness, light;
And where there is sadness, joy.
O Divine Master, grant that
I may not so much seek

To be consoled as to console;
To be understood as to understand;
To be loved as to love;
For it is in giving that we receive;
It is in forgiving that we are forgiven;
And it is in dying that we are born to Eternal Life.
—St. Francis

(Note: In this last line you might also consider that the ego is dying so it can be reborn as Spirit, which represents your true identity and is eternal).

FEEL LIKE IT'S REAL

It was the popular television series *Star Trek: The Next Generation,* that first introduced the public to the notion of a "holodeck." This was an empty room with four walls. As you entered it, a computer program would transport you into any time, place, or scenario you wished to experience. You would simply show up dressed for the part, ready to act it out. When you were finished, you would say, "end program," and head home. Desires satisfied; wishes fulfilled.

Today, scientists are frantically working to see if they can actually build a holodeck. In the gaming industry, systems like the Wii are heading us in that direction. But you have another option: You can begin using a kind of holodeck here and now. It's called your imagination. You see, you don't have to have everything you desire. You can just enjoy it through your imagination. You don't have to materialize it in the physical world—unless, of course, Spirit wants you to have it. Then Spirit will help attract it to you. And the truth is, you already have it anyway! When you are in a state of unity, you can look at someone or something and enter a state of what philosopher Joseph Campbell calls "ascetic arrest." In this state you simply appreciate and admire the beauty or other quality of whatever is before you. You don't have to possess or own it. This is why when you use the law of attraction in a spiritual way, you actually desire less in your life, not more. Sure, if it is your ultimate destiny to attract a lot of wealth to you, then you need to spend it on something. Go ahead and enjoy the nice home and automobile. Just be sure to appreciate it and not pervert it. Also remember that even if you feel you don't have anything, you already have it all as Spirit. Simply appreciate everything around you in this world.

Feeling Good versus Feeling Right

Though it is true that the more you feel good about attracting something, the more you increase the odds of getting it, unfortunately, I have known people who have distorted the idea advocated in *The Secret* that you should only do what feels good to you from this point on in your life. Whether intended by the contributing authors or not, some people have used this idea as a means to abnegate their responsibilities, helping them to justify how their egos should be self-indulgent, even "feeling good" about cruel and even criminal behavior. Here are some examples: "Hey, being a parent doesn't feel good. I think I will just abandon my kids." Or, "I don't have to put in a full day's work for the money my employer is giving me. It doesn't feel good. I'll play around on the Internet instead." Or, "Going to the bar every night and having three to four drinks makes me feel *really* good. I love this law of attraction stuff. I can drink all I want from now on."

Because of how dangerous the distortions to just do what "feels good" are, it is important to consider that maybe your soul doesn't so much want you to do what feels good as to do what feels right! When you engage in something that feels right, it may not even feel very good at all. Still, you will feel good about it in the long run, because you are doing good and that's the point.

So, if you are burned out as a parent, get a sitter and take a vacation! If you are no longer motivated by what you do for a living, find a different line of work. If life has gotten difficult and overwhelming, solve your problems by feeling your feelings instead of numbing them with alcohol. Stay conscious! Your feelings are a powerful gift to you. And don't forget to use the law of attraction to attract to yourself a deeper understanding of what your feelings are trying to tell you so you can infuse your emotions with the power of your soul, remaining open and sensitive and embracing all of life around you.

> *When you use the law of attraction, instead of focusing on what feels good, focus on what feels right! Feel good by doing good.*

SPIRIT STORY
Hair Envy

I am reminded of a young woman I will call Maggie. She was a student in a workshop I gave years ago. She loved long hair and desired to possess thick and luxurious locks. But her own hair was not suited to a long length, so she had always kept it short. Instead of just embracing her hair as fine the way it was, Maggie felt envious any time she would see a woman with especially beautiful long hair. In her jealousy, she would even imagine cutting off all of the woman's hair with scissors! When she told me, we both laughed for a bit at this notion (laughter is a sign of not taking a thought or feeling too seriously). Then I encouraged her to try another approach. I asked Maggie the next time she saw a woman with long, beautiful hair to remind herself that she is Spirit and so is everyone around her. Therefore, the other woman out there was really she. In short, as Spirit, Maggie could look at another woman and declare to herself, "Oh, my! What beautiful, long hair I have!" The same could be done for anything or anyone that creates jealousy within you. For example, you could say, "Oh, my! Look how well I paint as Vincent van Gogh!" Or, "What a beautiful home I have over there on the Pacific Ocean!" Or, "I sure have a wonderful sense of style. As a fashion model, look how well I dress!" Or, "I sure do love driving that sports car. What fun it is!" The examples are limitless.

TAP INTO YOUR FEELINGS
Key Insights

1. Every feeling has a gift to give you, and all feelings are your friends.

2. Emotional mastery helps you attract what you need to fulfill soul needs, not ego needs.

3. Remember, as a soul, you don't have to possess something. You can simply feel or imagine that you possess it. As you will discover, the feeling alone is often enough to satisfy you.

4. When you use the law of attraction, instead of focusing on what feels good, focus on what feels right! Feel good by doing good.

Chapter 10

Step 8
Highlight the Shadow in Others

In previous chapters, I illustrated how thoughts and feelings create. I also shared how you do not live in your own isolated world of thought or feeling. The thoughts, opinions, and speech of others have the power to impact and influence you for better or worse—and so do other people's misdirected emotions. This is important to understand because frequently in the manifestation process, people fail to get what they want because they do not understand how to manage the thoughts, feelings, and actions of those around them. Resistance happens, even resistance to the good that is trying to emerge. This is why you should know the following:

Evil *is* live *spelled backward,*
and evil does exist in this world.

Evil Refuses to Die

A spiritual teacher once gave me the most useful definition of evil I have ever heard: "Evil was once a great good that has outlived its usefulness and refuses to die." For thousands of years, war, murder, and abuse, for example, were pretty much the way to go for the human race. Conquerors from Alexander the Great to Napoleon marched into battle to win land, slaves, wealth, and possessions. They raped and pillaged all they wanted—to the acclaim of others. (That is, unless you were not on the winning end. Then you simply had to find your own conquering hero and look for the opportunity to take out your revenge.) What is extraordinary about the time we live in is how human beings as a whole no longer want these kinds of heroes. Hitler was just doing what lots of marauding warriors had done before him. So were Saddam Hussein, Idi Amin, Milosevic, and others. Only this time humanity didn't treat them as heroes, but as villains. Why? Because the soul of humanity is expanding its consciousness to move beyond egotistical power and domination as primary virtues to those of love, understanding, wisdom, and compassion.

The old dominate-and-conquer story is not going away easily though, which is why many loving, compassionate, intelligent, and kind souls are struggling to end this long legacy of abuse by helping people become conscious of another way of being. As they are attempting to do this, plenty of good, innocent, and decent people are being subjected to abuse and other horrible circumstances in life. Some have deliberately put themselves in harm's way to fend off the abuse around them. Others are simply naive, innocent victims who get caught up in the crossfire. They neither thought about the evil they were contending with nor attracted it into their lives. But the soul has put them there, so they must cope with it nevertheless. As they cope with it, they are also learning something everyone needs to understand. Old states of consciousness that are no longer useful (now anti-life or evil) often don't go away easily. And they frequently don't go out without a heavy-duty fight.

The function of evil is to block conscious growth and to try to stop the movement toward a greater good.

SPIRIT SPARK
Transforming Old States of Consciousness

The movie *Emmanuel's Gift* is an inspiration for overcoming an old state of consciousness. Emmanuel is a disabled man who lives in Ghana, West Africa. In a country where those with disabilities are frequently treated as outcasts or left to die, Emmanuel decided to change the way the disabled were viewed. Despite having only one leg, he rode a bicycle across Ghana, encouraging the disabled and others to view themselves as valuable contributors to society. Through determination, dignity, and courage, Emmanuel made a difference and changed the hearts and minds of those he came into contact with, not only in Ghana, but around the world.

EVIL VERSUS LIVE

So, how do you cope with the evil in this world? Do you simply ignore it? Do you choose to isolate and insulate yourself so you don't have to recognize it out there? If the soul wants you to be conscious of Spirit, and Spirit is in everything, then ignoring evil is hardly the responsible thing to do. Only by learning to recognize, eliminate, and transmute evil can the soul manifest more love and compassion in the world. Quite often that is the more difficult thing to do. Gandhi, Martin Luther King Jr., and others have lost their lives in the attempt to do so. History is filled with examples of noble individuals who sacrificed to help bring about a greater good.

An example of how I used to use the law of attraction to ignore the possibility of evil follows. Not too long after I learned about the law of attraction in the 1980s, I engaged in a practice of leaving my car unlocked. I was simply affirming and attracting to myself that I was safe no matter where I decided to go. One of my roommates at the time was a Christian woman who had also been a missionary. She observed my practice for some time before she took me aside and said calmly, "Thou shalt not tempt the Lord thy God." Naturally, I thought she had pretty limited thinking and could use a law of attraction course herself. Since that time, I have matured. I now recognize that it is not so much God I was tempting, but others. It's not that I believe we should live in a constant state of fear and mistrust—that is not what I choose to create with my own thoughts—but we can live in a world of love and freedom and be prudent at the same time. In the Muslim faith, they say, "Trust in Allah, but tie your camel." This is what my roommate was trying to convey: Trust in God, but lock your car!

As a natural mystic and a positive person dedicated to living a loving and compassionate life, it has been difficult for me to acknowledge the dark side of the world. I have since learned that the function of light is to help illuminate the dark. Learning to see yin and yang, the light and dark, and the good and evil has slowly turned me into a more well-rounded person. I still believe in the basic goodness of all human beings, but my psychological and spiritual training has helped me understand a lot about why people engage in negative behaviors. Slowly, I have discovered the value of spotting both the positive and the negative inclinations in others. Though I have taken a long time to accept it, I now firmly believe the following:

> *Whether conscious of it or not,*
> *others may attempt to sabotage your desires*
> *so they can benefit themselves instead of you.*

DIFFUSING NEGATIVITY

Here is a great technique to help you diffuse the negativity in others. At first it will seem awkward, but the more you practice it, the more automatic it will become.

1. **Focus in Front of Your Forehead.** Whether we know it or not, when we are in a detached and objective space, we tend to lift our attention to this spot. You might even find your eyes moving slightly together in an expression of curiosity or puzzlement as you place your attention here.

2. **Cross Your Arms If Necessary.** This protects your stomach region from the blast of negative energy coming your way.

3. **Breathe Slowly from Your Diaphragm.** This will help you remain centered and thoughtful, despite the way the other person is acting toward you.

4. **Affirm the Soul in Yourself and the Other.** By engaging the soul, you bring in its power and insight to help you deal effectively, firmly, and compassionately with the situation.

5. **Quietly Inquire.** In effect, you are practicing a form of the Watch and Listen technique as you calm your mind, observe what is happening, and inquire into the situation. Questions can include: Why is this person communicating with such emotional intensity? Is this negative upset really about me? What is this person really saying or needing at this moment?

6. **Firmly Respond.** In a safe, appropriate, firm, and dignified way, respond to the person in front of you. If a

person is being abusive with their negativity, you might say, "Enough! I am willing to listen to you and meet your needs if I can, but not until you calm down." If the person is just upset, you might respond as follows: "You are really upset (or hurt, or afraid), aren't you? Did you have a bad day? Do you need someone to talk to? Calm down. I am here for you."

7. **Visualize Healing.** Some people imagine the person who is being negative being surrounded by blue-white light. Others imagine a spiritual teacher or angels entering into the situation to assist. At times, I have visualized the person as a small, helpless child who needs support. Use whatever method works for you. Don't forget to send healing energy to yourself, too.

OVERCOMING RESISTANCE

Please remember that my belief of how others may try to sabotage you has come to me only after years of thinking and attempting to manifest just the opposite. In recognizing the reality of this, I do not expect others to sabotage me; I am simply more conscious of how they might. Of course, this could easily turn into a pessimistic and paranoid stance if you are not careful. And the goal of thinking this way is not to feed the negative, but to deflect it. A simple example comes to mind.

Let's say you decide to lose weight and want to train your body to desire healthier foods and enjoy exercise more. Using the law of attraction, you might begin by using an affirmation like, "Each and every day, I will learn to enjoy healthier foods and exercise." Then, you use visualization to stimulate your emotional desire-body to want to look a certain way, such as slim, fit, and strong. Everything is progressing wonderfully, and then suddenly the "environment" around you kicks up a bit. Your friends, partner, coworkers, parents, or children suddenly start to worry that you may be getting just a little too fit and good-looking for their comfort zone. Maybe they offer you some sweets to try to deflect you, or they buy you your favorite dessert. They may also tell you how great you look, so why bother losing weight?

By being aware of how others might resist your attempts to attract a greater good to yourself, you prepare yourself in a positive way for this very kind of resistance or sabotage. You understand that this is just part of the process, and in being conscious of this, you know how to handle it well. That leads us to this lesson:

> *Learning to work skillfully and harmoniously
> with the resistance in others is essential if you are
> to be a manifestor of Spirit in this world.*

In this example, maybe the skill you need is to avoid the people who might attempt to stop you from being as healthy as you want to be. You could also learn to graciously deflect them, thanking them for their point of view or the dessert, but turning it down regardless. You might even invite them to join you, creating a contest or team effort to see who can be the most fit in a month or two. You could also apply the law of attraction by affirming something like, "More and more, I am surrounded by fit and healthy people who support me in my goals."

CREATING A BETTER WORLD

The beauty of learning how to work this way with the resistance in others is how it prepares you to become an agent of Spirit in even larger circumstances. Shortly before sitting down to write this book, I was working on a special kind of movie review for a company I own called LoveMovies! These Empowerment Movie

Reviews demonstrated to others how movies could be watched in a more conscious way to increase our understanding of love in the world. I was reviewing the movie *Amazing Grace,* which highlights the efforts of William Wilberforce to abolish the slave trade in England and, by default, throughout Europe. What was most impressive about the film was his steady and persistent effort throughout the years to soulfully educate others about the horrors of slavery and how no human of good conscience could even remotely pretend to justify it. To stand for his cause, despite public ridicule and great emotional and physical suffering, was more than admirable. It was a lesson in precisely what we all need to master ourselves.

If we are truly here to build a better world the way Wilberforce sought to do, then we must become true warriors of Spirit. Through the weapons of intelligence, persistence, courage, truth, and an intention to be harmless, we need to cast our light in the darkness until others who are lost can be found and those who are blind can learn to see (to paraphrase the lyrics of the song, "Amazing Grace," which inspired the film).

SPIRIT SPARK
What's Stopping You?

It might appear that people out there are stopping you from attracting and manifesting a better life for yourself. But ultimately, it is your task to attract and embody enough soul qualities in yourself that you can be a force for good and positive change, no matter what is going on in the world. As Albert Einstein said, "The world is a dangerous place, not because of those who do evil, but because of those who look on and do nothing." Make sure you are not one of those who look on and do nothing in this world!

In an earlier chapter, I stated my curious dismay when first learning about the ends some people focus the law of attraction on. I asked myself, *Are we all meant to have beach houses in the world, or is there something more we can learn to desire and attract to ourselves in our stay here on Earth?* Attracting comfort, security, and a nice life is more than understandable. But if that is all everyone thought about, there would be no Gandhis, Wilberforces, Martin Luther King Jrs., Nelson Mandelas, Dalai Lamas, and Mother Teresas in this world. Neither would there be a Jesus or a Buddha to speak of.

How fortunate the human family is to have been blessed by the fact that these individuals used the law of attraction to create something of real service for others, even if it meant a great deal of personal sacrifice for themselves. How wise they were to understand that there would be forces attempting to resist them. Yet with skill, dignity, grace, and humanity, they continued to cast their lights so everyone could live in a better and brighter world. By emulating them, you can also help to drive out the darkness that exists in this world through the light, love, and power of the soul.

SPIRIT STORY
Working with the Negativity in Others

Becky was at a loss. She and her father had never seen things the same way. For most of her life, she felt criticized and verbally abused by him. As a child, she had no choice but to cope with it as best she could. As an adult, she learned to just get away and to go home as rarely as she could. Now that her father was much older, Becky wanted to find another way to get along. She wanted to transform the relationship. So, she started a campaign of regularly e-mailing her father on areas where they had common ground (the weather, good places to eat, how the children/grandchildren were, and so forth). Though Becky never had the kind of close relationship she had always wanted with her father, at least she established one where there were some points of connection. And by the time her father passed away, she felt love in her heart for what he was able to bring to her life instead of the constant bitterness and pain she had known before.

HIGHLIGHT THE SHADOW IN OTHERS
Key Insights

1. *Evil* is *live* spelled backward, and evil does exist in this world.

2. The function of evil is to block conscious growth and to try to stop the movement toward a greater good.

3. Whether conscious of it or not, others may attempt to sabotage your desires so they can benefit themselves instead of you.

4. Learning to work skillfully and harmoniously with the resistance in others is essential if you are to be a manifestor of Spirit in this world.

Chapter 11

Step 9
Remove the Shadow from Yourself

Just as others may block your ability to get what you want in life, you can also be your own worst enemy and stop the process yourself. There are a variety of ways you do this. You may not be aligned with your soul, use your mind effectively, or handle your emotions well. Maybe you have limiting beliefs or "stories" that stop you from moving forward in a more positive and constructive way. Ignorance and innocence may also be factors. As I have said before, some events just happen. You may not have manifested or created them with your thought processes, be they good or bad. But when these events arrive in your life, it is up to you to become more conscious and give yourself the opportunity to create either a soul or ego story.

BEING PROACTIVE VERSUS BEING REACTIVE

In my early years working with traumatized individuals, I experienced firsthand how victims of trauma (gang violence, poverty, abuse, rape, and incest) could react very differently to events. Some would handle the experience with courage, dignity, and strength. Others would collapse and react in a negative way, even if the adverse situations were not nearly as traumatic as those encountered by the people sitting next to them. What was the difference?

Stephen R. Covey, in his book *The 7 Habits of Highly Effective People,* offers some explanation. He talks about taking a proactive versus a reactive stance in life. Covey's proactive stance is similar to creating a soul story, and his reactive stance is like creating an ego story. The movie character Forrest Gump is an example. He is able to be proactive despite many hardships in his life (including mental and physical disabilities and not having a father). Forrest's resilience and his ability to be proactive come about in part due to the powerful loving impact his mother had on him. And it may have been for an additional reason. Maybe some people, like Forrest, are just born more soulful than others. Maybe they just come into this world with a greater measure of spiritual wisdom and maturity, no matter what kind of environment or life circumstances they are born into.

Recently, some scientists have argued that this is in fact the case. They even claim to have located "spiritual genes" that incline some individuals to be more soulful. But not everyone acts in a spiritual or proactive way. Far too often people stay stuck in their ego stories. This happens because every behavior, even seriously dysfunctional ones, brings a "payoff" at some level. People are rarely motivated to let go of those behaviors until that payoff ends, which is why the following is very important for you to understand:

If you are not careful, your unconscious and subconscious impulses may sabotage you.

THE LAW OF REPULSE

Spiritual training, the creation of soul stories, and learning to want payoffs that no longer feed ego behavior all help you drown out your ego stories. The techniques of surrendering to Spirit, aligning with the soul, and focusing on contribution all help you to live a better life. It would be great if all of this were easy to understand and cultivate in life. So why is it still so difficult? There are many reasons, but here is one:

> *Knowing what you don't want*
> *is as important as knowing what you do want.*
> *Learn to use both the*
> *law of attraction and the law of repulse.*

In short, you either don't see or understand what is stopping you (it is unconscious) or you only see it in a hazy kind of way (subconscious). Much of the work in learning to use the law of attraction in a more productive way isn't just affirming more of what you want, visualizing your desires, learning to be more grateful, or applying some of the other very useful techniques associated with law of attraction work. It is an understanding that somewhere within you—known or unknown—your ego, or misdirected thoughts or emotions, is keeping you from getting what you want or from knowing how to want what Spirit wants for you. How do you get more conscious so you can free yourself?

Ironically, one way is not to apply the law of attraction but to take up the law of repulse. I was exposed to the law of repulse more than fifteen years ago when going through a metaphysical course. It stated a very obvious fact that I had actually become aware of as early as grade school. All magnets have two poles. One side of the magnet attracts and the other side repels! This means that the law of attraction and the law of repulse always exist together. And there is as much power and opportunity in learning how to use the "no" side of the law of repulse as there is in using the "yes" side of the law of attraction.

This assertion differs from *The Secret,* which states that whenever you use the phrase "don't want," you always "want it." This is almost equivalent to saying that anytime you say "no," you really mean "yes"! Rapists who think their victims shouting "no" really do mean "yes" would be overjoyed in hearing this assumption! That is precisely why this statement is dangerous. Sometimes "no" can mean *no!* And, "don't want" can mean you really *don't want it!* It reminds me of a *Star Trek* episode where the *Enterprise* is under attack from photon torpedoes from another ship. What does the captain of the *Enterprise* say? He says, "Raise the shields!" In other words, he is saying, "*No! We don't want* the attack and we are not going to allow it to damage our ship." And because he is able to keep the shields up to implement the law of repulse, he is able to repel the photon torpedoes and keep the ship safe. That's why the law of repulse is a good thing to know and use.

Don't Wants and Do Wants

There is a partial truth to *The Secret*'s claim that "don't want" means you want it, but the assertion needs more clarification. *The Secret* states, "The only reason people don't have what they want is because they are listening to what they don't want instead of what they do want." In other words, they are only working with the law of repulse and are neglecting the other end of the magnetic pole that utilizes the law of attraction. Yes, it is true that knowing what you want as well as what you don't want is important. Being able to articulate what you want in a clear way helps attract it to you. You are now more conscious about what you want and can get clear on how to look for it.

But there is also power in the "don't want" side. Some law of attraction coaches know this, which is why they have you start out by articulating clearly what you don't want as a way of stimulating greater thought about what you do want. For example: I don't want another abusive relationship; I do want a loving, caring, and compassionate partner. I don't want this dead-end job; I do want a more rewarding and fulfilling career. I don't want to struggle with money all the time; I do want to have enough to meet my needs with extra money in the bank. I don't want these photon torpedoes to attack the ship; I do want to find a way to keep the ship safe! Both the "don't want" and the "do want," the "no" and the "yes," help you clarify your subconscious and unconscious desires and impulses. Both help bring them into the light of day. Therefore, learning to use both is important. Knowing what you don't want helps you stop wanting it. Knowing what you do want helps you know how to want it even more.

Of course, there is no shame in the fact that you may not have known about the law of attraction or the law of repulse and how to use each well. That is what the unconscious is all about: It is the part of you that doesn't know what you don't know. The subconscious is the part of you that only kind of knows, but isn't totally sure yet. That brings me to another point about how you may stop yourself. As I have said before, sometimes events just happen, and you don't manifest them at all. You may also be entirely unaware of how to cope with these events because they are so new to your experience. No, you did not attract them to yourself (though maybe the soul attracted them to you for the sake of spiritual growth). And yes, you are here to learn how to cope with the events you encounter more consciously and effectively. Until then, you need to understand that:

Ignorance and innocence may exist
within you, creating a lack of skill
in manifesting what you want
and blocking you from working
more effectively in the world.

THE SHADOW OF THE LAW OF ATTRACTION

Ah, yes! The law of attraction. Finally, you know the "secret" to getting whatever you want in life. But what you wish for can all too often be driven by your ego. Maybe you are conscious of the selfishness and tentative morality of your ego's wishes, or maybe you are not because they exist at a more subconscious (only slightly aware) or unconscious (not aware at all) level. Still, wishing from the ego can get you into trouble. Here's how:

1. **The Downfall Wish.** Yes, it looks good on the surface, but over time you realize your wish carries the seeds of your own demise! Like that relationship that looked good at first, until you discovered that the other person had problems like emotional instability, control issues, hidden agendas to manipulate you or take something of value from you (money, dignity, health), and so forth. Remedy? Next time, wish for the soul quality of discernment instead!

2. **The Covet Wish.** Covet means a desire to have something or someone belonging to another person. Instead of attempting to attract the partner, business, reputation, or child that is rightfully yours, you use the law of attraction as a sneaky way to steal these from another person. Remedy? Establish a spiritual identity. Cultivate ethics and spiritual values. Get more secure that you can attract what is rightfully meant for you instead of trying to take it from another person.

3. **The Greedy Wish.** Like Mickey Mouse in "The Sorcerer's Apprentice" from the movie *Fantasia,* you wish for something that ends up being far more than you can handle. Witness how many lottery winners

blow all of their cash, or how some famous people burn out under the spotlight, or attractive people discover they can't handle the attention and become vain and superficial. Remedy? Practice the ONE steps I have given you to orient toward Spirit, negate the ego, and engage the soul.

4. **The Evil Wish.** Here you either manipulate someone else into wanting something that ends up not being good for them or you wish evil directly on someone out of jealousy, cruelty, or a need for revenge. Remedy? Follow all of the remedies mentioned above. And remember, karma does work. You can't escape the negative consequences of your evil wishes for long.

Yes, sometimes you just may not know any better! That's okay, too! And, your motives may also be mixed up, especially if you have two competing urges or are just flat-out confused. Remember the saying, "Ask for milk and get the whole cow"? Working with the law of attraction can be like this, especially if you don't have the power of your mind and soul developed enough to know how to manifest more positive results in the world. For example, a child may crave attention from a parent, but that hardly means the child desires to be sexually abused! To imply the child "manifested" or somehow wanted to be molested is dangerous and destructive. The child simply doesn't know better. She is ignorant and innocent. In my humble opinion, law of attraction teachings should never be used to make a child, or an adult, feel guilty about these kinds of misunderstandings or confusions.

Looking at another example, let's say you are busy creating your "wish list" of what you do and don't want in a potential spouse or partner. Maybe you put good-looking, financially successful, kind, funny, sexy, and fun on your list. You attract just such a person into your life. Only you may also attract things you just didn't even know to watch out for like a narcissistic personality disorder that you only see more clearly after you have suffered under this person's particular brand of abuse. Once you become aware of these kinds of behaviors, you can use the law of repulse to get the heck out of there. Then, you can use the law of attraction again and be even smarter in your next choice.

Another dilemma with being unconscious, subconscious, ignorant, and innocent is how often you may not see yourself as others see you. This can include both the light and the shadow side of your personality. An example of not seeing your shadow may be believing you are great with money when you are really engaged in reckless spending. Another example is thinking you do not have to worry about your health when all of your biological indicators (cholesterol, blood pressure, and so forth) suggest that you are on your way to contracting a life-threatening disease. An example of not seeing the light can come from being overly harsh and critical of yourself, or believing that you are worthless and have no talent, even when others try to show you the opposite and tell you quite bluntly, "Yes, you do!"

If you strive to be conscious, if you want to use the power of your mind and soul correctly, you need to do everything you can to ask for (or attract) a clear understanding of what you are really like so you can see your strengths and weaknesses as they really are. This brings about humility. True humility is not putting yourself down if you really do have a gift. It is not hyping yourself up if you actually lack certain qualities you think you possess. Humble people are gracious and easy to be around because they know who they are and can appraise correctly what they are good at and what they are not. They know when to do something themselves and when to delegate a task. And they know how to see the true gifts and talents of others in comparison to their own. Until you have that clear understanding of what you are really like (and how many of us do?), it is valuable to be firm with your ego so you can overcome your negative tendencies and gentle where you need to be so you can stay open to compassion, love, and self-respect. It is also important to remember the following:

> *Forgive yourself for failing*
> *to attract what you believe*
> *you want and need. Then realign*
> *with your soul and Spirit,*
> *and once again proceed.*

SPIRIT SPARK
How Others See You

Want to be really courageous? Take a journey back in time and ask people who knew you how they really thought and felt about you. That's what Harry does in the popular movie *Something's Gotta Give*. A womanizer, Harry finally meets his match in Erica, a woman his own age who is bright, savvy, mature, and full of heart and soul. Harry follows through with his typical commitment-phobic pattern and runs from the relationship with Erica, only to feel heartbroken over having lost her. To win her back and understand himself more clearly, he looks up every woman he has ever known and asks for their frank perceptions of what it was like to be with him. Most of what Harry hears is far from pleasant, but by exposing the shadow in himself and bringing it into the light of the soul, Harry becomes a better potential partner to the woman he loves.

Forgiveness keeps you open to the process of learning and growing. It helps you be patient with your mistakes while you attempt to be more conscious each and every day. As for the attempt to realign with your Spirit, forgiveness helps you remember that you are not alone in this world. Some people claim that we all are children of this universe. By keeping the faith in yourself and others, you can continue to remove the obstacles from your life, helping you to attract a better future for yourself and everyone around you.

SPIRIT STORY
Listening with Heart

Jim had heard it all before—all the reasons why his wife Susan was too sick and depressed to get a job. They didn't have children, and Jim really wanted Susan to contribute to the family income. She once worked as a nurse, but a back injury had sidelined that, and for nearly two years she spent most of her days feeling depressed and lonely. Every time Jim looked at her, he felt hurt and angry. Their conversations had also deteriorated into either fighting or resigned silence. One day, Jim had the insight that maybe some of Susan's unhappiness was due to his attitude toward her. Seeing this he started a daily practice wherein he would pray that Susan would find happiness and peace despite her condition. And when he talked to her, he made an attempt to be more patient and to remember how much he had once loved this woman, especially before the injury. To Jim's amazement, after two months of his behaving in this way, Susan announced that she wanted to get a job. Jim continued his practice and within a few more months, Susan was employed as a notary and much happier than she had been in some time. Their relationship also improved. Though it wasn't quite like it was before Susan got hurt, the dark cloud over them lifted, and the fighting all but ceased. Most of all, Jim learned to work with the shadow of his own negative thoughts and to communicate in a more loving and compassionate way.

REMOVE THE SHADOW FROM YOURSELF
Key Insights

1. If you are not careful, your unconscious and subconscious impulses may sabotage you.

2. Knowing what you don't want is as important as knowing what you do want. Learn to use both the law of attraction and the law of repulse.

3. Ignorance and innocence may exist within you, creating a lack of skill in manifesting what you want and blocking you from working more effectively in the world.

4. Forgive yourself for failing to attract what you believe you want and need. Then realign with your soul and Spirit, and once again proceed.

Chapter 12

Step 10
Execute and Easy Does It!

Congratulations! You've reached the last step. By this stage, you have learned to make sure you are being guided by Spirit. You have received thoughts and ideas of what Spirit wants for you in meditation. You have ordered these thoughts into a coherent game plan of how to proceed to attract and manifest what Spirit wants for you. And you have learned how to manage your emotions in such a way that you decrease the odds they will abort what you are trying to accomplish and increase the odds for success! So far, so good. Now it is time to master one final process. You have to act to make it so. You have to build a runway so the plane carrying what you want can land and those wonderful ideas can deplane and enjoy their new home.

Prepare for Turbulence

Hopefully, building that runway will be a smooth process. But be prepared for a few bumps in the road. I remember attending a Lamaze class and watching idyllic videos of mothers having their babies. One mother's child seemed to just swim out of the woman's womb while entering the warm tub of water she was being birthed into. Another child simply slid out of the mother like someone had magically greased the birth canal with pure virgin olive oil so that the baby could just glide into the arms of the joyful father. He, in turn, presented the child to the mother, who looked like she hadn't broken a sweat.

Yep! Everyone in that class was primed and ready to attract birth experiences just like those in the videos. But, you know, the best-laid plans don't often work out that way. For example, how did I know that after coaching my unborn son to emerge from the womb to a blissful piece of violin music that his father would get so nervous with the birth experience that he wouldn't be able to get the CD player to work? (I swear my son was saying inside me, "Hey, Mom! When are you going to play that tune?") Naturally, when we had our Lamaze class reunion six months later, we all discovered that no one had managed to manifest a birth experience like the ones in those videos, even though many of us tried to coach ourselves into having similar blissful episodes.

Even the best-laid plans may not
turn out as you intend,
so be open to the element
of surprise as you go.

Sure, sometimes when the plane lands, it hits the runway so smoothly that you wonder if you have even touched down. (While traveling to Hawaii once, my plane did land that way. The passengers were so amazed nearly everyone broke into spontaneous applause!) But most of the time there is a little turbulence in the air or a few bumps as the plane makes contact. I attended a real-estate training course once, and the presenters used this plane metaphor for agents selling homes. They instructed the agents to give their clients small wooden airplanes along with a list of things that could go wrong in the buying and selling process. If the clients exclaimed what a smooth experience it had been when the home closed escrow, the agent could gently remind them that they should have been in the cockpit, where all of the action was—meaning that the agent had acted like the pilot, handling all kinds of turbulence in such a way that it still seemed like a smooth ride.

Overcome Obstacles

Now, I'm not trying to scare you away. I'm just trying to remind you that, even if you have Spirit as the pilot, have a great idea and game plan, and know how to stay poised and confident in your emotions, there still may be some obstacles you need to hurdle. That's why knowing how to skillfully manage obstacles can help you not only be prepared, but work through them.

I am reminded of the movie *The Pursuit of Happyness* based on the true story of Chris Gardner. One of the most impressive things is not just how dedicated Chris was to his son or how he managed to go from rags to riches, but how he navigated obstacle after obstacle in a determined way to manifest his dream of being able to provide for his son as a stockbroker. In short, he practiced two qualities that are absolutely essential to the manifestation process: *patience and persistence!* Without these two items in your tool kit, you may as well get ready to circle your plane in the air for a long time to come. Or you might have to go through a crash landing. You may even give up flying altogether. That's why it's necessary to cultivate the poise, stamina, and determination to make the changes you need—so that Spirit can at last deliver on Earth all the heaven it has in store for you.

Another important quality to constantly cultivate in the final stages of manifestation is *harmlessness.* Especially when the pressure is on due to the natural stresses of attempting to finally attract what you desire, it is easy for your ego to kick up in a number of ways. Mentally, you may need to monitor becoming critical of yourself and others in a non-helpful way if things don't go according to plan. You may need to guard against arrogance and pride if you perceive yourself as better than others now that you know you will obtain what you desire. Emotionally, fear and anger can emerge if you think you might lose something that is almost in your grasp. Because of these temptations remember to stay oriented toward Spirit and maintain detachment and divine indifference in addition to remaining harmless.

You can also sabotage the execution process through the misuse of speech. Words are powerful; they help to create the world around us. Even God in the Jewish Torah and the Christian Bible is said to have created the world through the power of the spoken word. So be careful. When you talk too much about what you are trying to attract or you share your ideas and inspirations with too many people and too soon, you end up depleting the attraction process. You have probably already experienced this.

Have you ever gotten tired when someone was talking too much? Instead of attracting your attention, that person may actually have started to repel you! You probably also know what it is like to get a new idea, share it with someone, and watch that person take it away from you. Now, maybe this happened because it wasn't really your idea to manifest in the first place. Maybe Spirit gave it to you to share with someone else because Spirit felt that person had more skill for manifesting it at the time than you did. But, if it *was* yours to manifest, then it means you lacked the wisdom to know when and with whom to share it. That is why silence is often encouraged in the attraction process; remain silent until you are absolutely certain you are sharing with the right people, in the right place, and at the right time. In short, practice *discernment.*

Patience, persistence, harmlessness,
and discernment are always valuable qualities,
but they are especially crucial at the
final stages of the law of attraction process.

BRING IT TO FULL TERM

How do you know if your idea is really ready to be born? Here are a few ways you can evaluate it:

1. **How thought-full is your idea?** Yes, some ideas just magically manifest. The stars all line up right, synchronicities happen all around, and everything just falls into place nicely. Actually, the manifestation of this book happened very much that way. Many elements (agent, publishing company, time alone to write it) just fell into place. But even with this boost, there was still the process of writing thoughts that hopefully would be of value to others. That's why even if it seems easy at times, be sure you are thought-full in your preparation as you manifest your desire.

2. **How valuable is your idea?** Sure, the idea thrills you, but will anyone else care about it? Yes, some ideas are so innovative that others may not catch on for some time, so why bother with their opinion? If you really don't care about sharing your idea or creative endeavor with others, then all that matters is that it has value to you. However, if your goal is to have others respond to it in a healthy way, then their needs and wants should be considered. Remember, the more others need or desire your idea, the more support and life they will bring to it.

3. **Does your idea light a fire?** Can it really catch on in such a way that others gladly feed the flames of enthusiasm over your idea? Will they spread the news of your idea to others so it will reach those who need it? Will they continue to respect your stewardship over it? Will they be able to take good care of it if you delegate certain aspects of the creative process to them? These questions and more are good to consider before you let your idea head out the door.

4. **How prepared are you for your idea?** Some people totally sabotage success because they are not at all prepared for the life changes it may bring them. This includes media attention, new ways old friends may feel about your success and perceive you, and financial wealth that comes knocking at your door. Sure, you've been busy attracting success, but have you also attracted to yourself the capacity to handle that success when it comes to you? Next time, make sure you do.

These questions are important to consider no matter what you are trying to attract, and they apply to a variety of situations. Pick one situation in your life, and see how they apply to you. Then practice applying them to as many situations as possible, until it becomes a habit to ask these four questions during any law of attraction or manifestation process.

Who's in the Delivery Room?

If you've ever had a baby or been in a delivery room during a birth, you know that a team is required to support the mother. Giving birth to anything can be hard work. Once you have manifested it, that new relationship, creative project, or business is going to require team effort to help sustain it. You might also need some time to adapt to the changes of finally getting what you want.

After I had my son, I didn't have a lot of support in coping with the massive changes. Fortunately, we had the means at the time to hire some help. I remember interviewing a woman who was from a Middle Eastern country for the job. She spoke about the cultural difference between a woman giving birth in her homeland and a woman giving birth here in the United States. In her country, she told me, a woman who had a baby was considered to have just performed a great service. For this reason, she was given a month to recover. During this time, other women in the community would cook and clean for her. She would be given daily massages to help her get back into shape. This recovery period also gave the mother plenty of time to bond with her child, and it gave other members of the community a chance to bond with the baby and mother.

What I took most from this story is that the hyper-individualism of the United States causes us to miss out on some really important processes whenever someone goes through a major transition. We have become too focused on the egotistical notion of "me" at the expense of the spiritual idea of "we." I don't know about you, but I like the idea of a team of people coming in to support me when I've just given birth to something. Think about other examples. How much healthier would your business be if you had a team of people ready to help it grow and prosper once you finally opened the door? Do you think you might manage a financial windfall better if you attracted a team of qualified and caring financial experts at the same time? Doesn't it feel better to attract a team of people who can help you stay focused on your fitness and health rather than attempting to go it all alone?

Whenever you give birth
to someone or something, it is beneficial
to have already attracted a good support team
to help your "baby" prosper as it grows.

Too often people forget the important steps to being prepared once they attract something into their lives. The next time you attempt to attract the car of your dreams, why not attract a really good auto shop to help you take care of it at the same time? Think about how many people get married or dive into relationships without having a clue regarding whom to talk to if they hit some trouble spots. A good relationship counselor might be handy to have around, too. Many people join networking groups precisely because they want to know "who they're gonna call" if something goes wrong. Sure, you can pick up the phone book and try to find someone at random. But isn't it better to set the intent to attract skilled people through qualified referrals right to your front door?

CYCLES OF MANIFESTING

At times, it seems to me that we live in a culture obsessed with the cycle of doing and are scared to death of the cycle of being. Think about it: Why do so many people view progress only as getting more and more of something? It's as if we only feel good about ourselves when we think we are climbing mountains. It has almost become a cardinal sin to sit around and "do nothing." I once had an interesting meditation on roller coasters. I thought to myself, *Why is it that on a roller coaster we typically think "ho-hum" while we are going up the hill and scream with delight when we are crashing down the steep slope? Why is it a sign of courage to face your fear on a roller coaster by throwing up your arms and screaming "Whee!" as you are hurtling toward the bottom? Most of all, why is it when we encounter the "downers" in real life that we fail to view them in the same way? How come we don't get a sensation of delight out of heading into unknown and scary territories, throwing up our arms and squealing "Yippee"?*

**Remember the manifestation process works
in cycles. After you have attracted something,
be ready to let something else go.
That way you make room for Spirit
to attract something more to you.**

SPIRIT SPARK
Cut the Cord

You've worked so hard! You've asked Spirit to guide you, come up with a well-thought-out plan, kept your emotions positive and constructive, and managed to keep your ego out of the way (well, most of the time). Finally, you are seeing the fruits of your labor. That relationship, business, new health discipline, financial investment, vacation, et cetera is finally yours! Only remember, even though you helped to attract it, ultimately it doesn't belong to you. That's why it's important at the time of birth to "cut the cord" to what you have created or manifested. Why? Because at some point others will start to have a say in what you have created. If you have manifested a relationship, family, or business, then your partner, children, and coworkers will have their own thoughts, wishes, and desires that will need to be considered and coordinated with your own. Birthing something is just the beginning. There's a long journey ahead. So, be sure you continue to practice the ONE, TWO, THREE techniques at every step of the way on your life's journey.

Just as climbing a mountain is similar to the process of attracting something, heading into a valley is a sign of letting go. Letting go helps you clear the way for attracting something more. And, letting go can be good for you if you know how to handle it well, which is why I've never understood the negative connotation around the word *depression*. To me, a depression is similar to a sponge that has become too heavy with water. To wring out the sponge, the person frequently needs a period of rest, contemplation, and orientation toward Spirit to sort out all that has just happened. Instead of allowing depressed individuals a cycle of "being," we tend to feed them Prozac so they can rapidly get back into a stage of doing. This is not to say that Prozac can't be helpful. If someone is in danger of being suicidal, medication may help him stabilize emotionally. But sadly, just like we shove mothers who have just had children rapidly back into the workplace, we shove people who need rest, healing, and contemplation too rapidly back into the *do* place.

Life is full of cycles. When you attract something, you may also need time to assimilate and digest it. And when you lose something you wanted to attract, it can also be an opportunity to clear out the old to make space for something new. Just as you breathe in and out, make a conscious effort to alternate between attracting and repelling, between doing and being. Understand that after you manifest anything, you begin the ONE, TWO, THREE cycle all over again. So hook back up to Spirit, throw up your arms, and say, "Yahoo!" whenever you feel you have lost something or when a situation didn't work out as you hoped it would. Let Spirit reinspire you. That way, you can start the law of attraction cycle all over again—and possibly something even better may be waiting for you.

SPIRIT STORY
The Power to Make It Happen

There are a number of people who really know how to manifest what they want in the world, but one I have admired for some time is Jack LaLanne, often called the "godfather of fitness." I first heard about Jack in my early twenties when I worked at one of his fitness centers. But years later, I had an opportunity to meet him in person, which rapidly explained to me why Jack has been able to overcome so many obstacles in his life and achieve so much success. I ran into Jack at the health food store. At the time I met him he was in his early eighties. To say he seemed much younger would be an understatement. I'm around plenty of vital, energetic young people, but Jack was radiating something unique and much more powerful than simply his youthful vitality. The only way I can think to describe it is that Jack possessed a kind of dynamic power that was totally saturated with positive energy.

Later I mused to myself that if I were a germ, or wanted to cling to any kind of negative mental or emotional state, coming within three feet of Jack would make me feel like I had met a spiritual "terminator," who was saying to my negative energy, "Resistance is futile!" I couldn't help but imagine that negativity withering away immediately or running away for its life. After meeting Jack I have always been inspired to learn more about how to flood my being with such positive energy. That is what I believed Jack had an abundance of, and it is something I encourage you to cultivate as well.

EXECUTE AND EASY DOES IT
Key Insights

1. Even the best-laid plans may not turn out as you intend, so be open to the element of surprise as you go.

2. Patience, persistence, harmlessness, and discernment are always valuable qualities, but they are especially crucial at the final stages of the law of attraction process.

3. Whenever you give birth to someone or something, it is beneficial to have already attracted a good support team to help your "baby" prosper as it grows.

4. Remember the manifestation process works in cycles. After you have attracted something, be ready to let something else go. That way, you make room for Spirit to attract something more to you.

Chapter 13

THREE Techniques

STEP 7

Tap into Your Feelings

As you continue to respond to what Spirit wants for you,
be aware of the various feelings that surface.
By inquiring into the need of the emotion
and changing your thinking,
you vibrate your feelings to a higher level.

As you may already know, but only somewhat appreciate, it is rarely a lack of inspiration or even thought that aborts the manifestation process. Time and again, things fall apart at the emotional level. Just take a moment to reflect. How frequently has something great blown up because someone became afraid and ran away from the process prematurely? How often has an unhealthy display of anger caused too much resentment and harm for people to continue to feel confident in creating something joyful and wonderful together? Or what about when jealousy breeds an unhealthy sense of competition and insecurity in people, making everything tense and causing upset instead of generating collaboration and appreciation? Even too much enthusiasm can become a problem. Just think of when people naively push something along without taking the time to clearly see if what is being created has a solid enough foundation to make it through the long run.

In recent years, there has been a greater understanding of how to work with emotions in a more intelligent and masterful way. Some spiritual texts assert that humans are primarily "kamamanas," or emotionally minded, in their approach. This means they feel and don't really think much at all. They react without taking time to understand what they are feeling and why. The cognitive therapies, neurolinguistic programming techniques, and more advanced law of attraction techniques all provide practical methods for dealing more effectively with emotional states. Books like the very popular *Excuse Me, Your Life Is Waiting* by Lynn Grabhorn and *Emotional Intelligence* by Daniel Goleman are also very useful.

Another popular law of attraction book, *The Amazing Power of Deliberate Intent* by Esther Hicks and Jerry Hicks, provides numerous examples of how to rethink an emotion so it can vibrate to a higher state. This is incredibly similar to the therapeutic training I received in rational emotive behavior therapy, where you learn to look at and change the many assumptions that underlie your feeling states so you can come to more rational and effective solutions for how you interpret events. Here is an example of this technique:

Changing Your Thoughts about a Feeling

Feeling: Overwhelmed

Debilitating Thoughts Underlying Feeling: I no longer have the energy I need to accomplish everything I want to get done. I am worried that I won't get everything done on time. Others will be upset with me. I don't know what to do.

Helpful Thoughts to Transform Feeling: I have managed to get things done on time before. I can find a way to do that again now. This isn't the first time I have felt overwhelmed in my life. I know I will come out all right this time as well.

The advantage to this technique is that it helps you create more rational and productive thoughts about the situation. This gives you more energy and orients you toward being more confident. But there is another way to take the process even deeper. Similar to inner-child psychology work, or the body-psychology technique of focusing, instead of trying to talk yourself into an improved emotional state, you simply allow the emotion to be exactly as it is and then inquire into it. In other words, you validate and acknowledge the feeling. You view it as trying to communicate something important to you, and do your best to ask questions of the feeling and listen to it accordingly.

Inquiring into an Emotional State

Feeling: Overwhelmed

Feeling Inquiry: What does this feeling need? What is it trying to communicate to me?

Intuitive Response to Inquiry (based on impressions you receive as the feeling attempts to communicate with you): I'm tired! I'm tired of all the pressure you put on me. You just drag me from one deadline to the next. And, of course, you always care what others will think about you. You never think about what I want. I'm sick of all your work. That is all you do! And you worry about what others think. When will it ever end? When will you just let go and relax? What about taking time for rest and play? If you don't listen to me at some point and not try to talk me out of this feeling of being overwhelmed yet again, your body is going to break down.

Where to Go from Here (based on asking the feeling to resolve the situation for you): I just want to know when you will also make time for rest and play. I want you to find a way to get more support from others so they will help lift the load. I also need proof that what others think and need doesn't always matter. Please show me that you matter, too!

Commitment to Change (based on your response after listening to and accepting what your feeling needs): You are right. I do need to take a break. I need to stop taking on so many assignments. I don't need to prove myself to others all the time. I can acknowledge that I am already enough. But I need to get through this assignment right now. I know you may not fully trust it, but I promise that if you cooperate with me a little longer, I will take that break right afterward. I will not take on any more assignments until I have had a chance to rest and play. Does that sound good to you?

This dialogue between yourself and the emotion could go on, especially if the feeling remains reactive and unheard. You will know the process is complete, however, when the feeling relaxes and moves of its own accord into alignment and not resistance. You will also probably feel a surge of physical energy due to the feeling's new sense of cooperation.

SPIRIT SPARK
Wipeout

If something you wanted to attract or manifest didn't get off the ground due to an emotional wipeout, here is a way to recover. Take some time to reflect on what happened. Then attempt to access the love of the soul. Enter into prayer or meditation, or relax your body as best you can and open up to the existence of love all around you. If you are praying to a particular spiritual individual, ask that person to fill you with the energy of love. If you have trouble relating in this individualized way, simply imagine that love is pouring into the pores of your skin and saturating your body. Allow yourself to be drenched in the energy of love. Let its healing and nurturing power sink into every cell of your being. Conclude the exercise when you feel that this has sufficiently taken place. Then go about the rest of your day.

STEP 8

Highlight the Shadow in Others

**Understand that as you implement
what Spirit wants for you, others
may not always react in a favorable way.
Notice and highlight what the resistance
in others may be, then cope with,
transform, or walk away as needed.**

One of the most difficult things to accept is that others may consciously or unconsciously be working in opposition to what you want to manifest. This is not always malicious. If two people are competing to win a race or both want to be rewarded at their jobs, it is simply a matter of two people attempting to do their best. It might appear that the other person is trying to stop you, but it is really a matter of both people trying to succeed, which is natural, healthy, and good.

However, there are certain circumstances where this is not the case. There are some dangerous elements and cruel people whom you can only deal with effectively by totally staying away from them. They are simply too dysfunctional, destructive, nonheroic, and egotistical in their way of being in the world. Until their souls have enough power to break through the hardened, ignorant, and cruel shells of their egos, there isn't much anyone can do.

Though walking away may seem easy, you may need to carefully plan out an exit strategy for real success. This is because running away from someone or something without a clear understanding of where you are running to may only get you into more trouble. It is better to prepare for your exit. Understand clearly why you are leaving. Get a support group to help you before, during, and after you leave. Prepare yourself financially, physically, emotionally, mentally, and spiritually. Then, there will be no regrets, and you will find yourself in a much better place after you go.

Next is the path of staying and trying to cope. Here you will learn a lot about your own strengths and weaknesses, including how the other person triggers you emotionally. You will discover all of the ways you get hooked mentally and fail to detach because you do not own your projections and dysfunctional ways of being that the other person triggers in you. You will also learn about how you may be setting off the other person by not being sensitive to his bad moods or by bringing things up in an awkward way due to your poor timing. You will even discover unrealistic ways in which you are expecting the person to change. The more you expect from the individual, the more disappointed you end up feeling. The more you fail to see that person clearly, the more muddled your reaction to him will be.

Finally, there is the rewarding, but often difficult path of redemption. As a counselor, a lot of my life has been dedicated to healing and helping people. At times, I have hung in there too long, attempting to heal people who aren't ready for it or who simply don't want to do the work on their own. Letting go and letting God has been a valuable lesson. If I can help, and others are willing to help themselves, so be it. If not, it is best to let them go! Keeping this in mind, know that when it comes to healing and redeeming others, the techniques are numerous. Some of my quick favorites include prayer and reinforcing the positive qualities people possess. Remaining centered, focused, and calm when others fail to act in the highest way also helps. At times, I even call upon the soul in myself and others to bring more love to all.

SPIRIT SPARK
Planetary Pain Body

What is the "pain body"? Eckhart Tolle, author of *A New Earth,* shares how the pain body is comprised of accumulated emotional pain that comes from holding on to negative emotional states over a long period of time. People with heavy pain bodies are addicted to drama in relationships, perpetuating a state of chronic unhappiness. Tolle shares how our media helps perpetuate this pain body by keeping people in a constant state of turmoil, anxiety, anger, and fear. War, prejudice, and the suppression of feminine values also keep the planetary pain body going. As you disidentify from your emotional body, you break free of its grip. And by no longer feeding it negative emotional images (movies, television), sounds (music with violent and degrading themes), and actions (oppressive and abusive actions of any kind), you help free the planetary pain body as well.

STEP 9

Remove the Shadow from Yourself

*Now take time to understand
the various ways you may be resisting
what Spirit wants for you. If need be,
ask others to assist you in removing
the various blocks you may have
to manifesting what Spirit wants.*

Many of the exercises in this book help you remove blocks from within yourself. But, at times, some blocks may be particularly stubborn and difficult because you typically don't even know they are there or how they are creating problems in your life. Good friends, or a long-term trusted relationship with a mentor (like someone who can give you spiritual guidance, coaching, or counseling), can be very useful here.

In a number of spiritual traditions, it is common to have mentors like these assigned to guide you. They not only help you deepen your connection to Spirit, they reveal where you are blocked mentally, emotionally, and physically. They observe what you don't see about yourself, both the positive and the negative. With compassion, they reflect this to you. At times this compassion may be delivered in a stern, "tough love" kind of way.

As a counselor, coach, and spiritual guide, I was often assigned people like these who aided me. At times, a group of people would even fill this role. At first, I was like most people and found myself shy, reticent, and at times defensive in this process. It took time to feel safe enough to open up and disclose some of my innermost thoughts, fears, and life experiences. Now I know the value of these kinds of mentors, and I actively seek them out to help me see what I am not aware of about myself. Presently, I have four such individuals who fill that role in my life, and I have had at least a dozen throughout my life.

Receiving this kind of feedback isn't always easy. That is why it is important to have a person you respect and trust give it to you. It helps if the individual knows how to deliver tough news you need to realize about yourself in a skillful way so you are truly open to listening. Some friends and intimate partners can do this, but in general, only people who are trained to deliver tough feedback with wisdom and compassion know how to do it well. This is why I strongly encourage you to attract a well-trained person into your life whose main function is to act as a spiritual guide, counselor, or coach. This can be a very valuable and unique kind of relationship, one that will really serve you in living a more peaceful and joyous life.

If you don't have access to an individual who can help you identify and remove your blocks, you can default to the following intuitive methods. Remember, you are trying to identify and see within yourself something you may not even know exists. You can access the intuition in various ways, but a favorite of mine is to consult an oracle or piece of sacred text. You simply ask a question and then look for clues to the answer. If you are using a sacred text, you can allow a piece of sacred scripture to enter your mind or you can close your eyes and let yourself be guided randomly to a piece of text in the book. If you are using a different kind of oracle, like cards with symbolic images, you can simply shuffle the deck and pull out one or more cards that may guide you.

Whatever method you choose, understand that you are working in an intuitive and symbolic way. The answers you receive are usually not definitive. More often, they offer hints that you can meditate on, pray about, or reflect upon in a journal or in your mind throughout your day. In time, the hints will offer greater clarity and direction that you can either discuss with someone or work with on your own to get deeper insight.

SPIRIT SPARK
Qualities of an Ideal Mentor

Here is a quick list of some qualities a good mentor will have:

1. Knowledge of you and various aspects of your life

2. Your best interests at heart

3. Skill in helping you to see and remove blocks

4. Specific expertise in your area of inquiry, such as relationships, business, parenting, spiritual guidance, health, finances, and so forth

5. Many of the soul qualities mentioned in chapter 3, Engage the Soul

---

STEP 10

Execute and Easy Does It!

*Aligned with Spirit and committed
to doing what Spirit wants,
execute your plan to attract what is needed
to be of service in some area of your life.
Remember to let it flow!
Keep Spirit involved in the process as you go.*

One of the most difficult things to remember during an attraction process is respecting the need to guard against fatigue. Fatigue comes at all levels: spiritual, egotistical, mental, emotional, and physical. If you are not careful to manage fatigue at these levels, what you are trying to attract will abort and show up half-baked or as a sluggish reflection of what you had really hoped for. The following tips can help you.

Spiritual Fatigue: This can come about when you strain in meditation to discover what Spirit wants you to attract. It can also happen when you worry too much about whether you are staying oriented toward Spirit and engaging your soul. To guard against spiritual fatigue during meditation, attempt to limit your meditation time to only twenty minutes a day. Inspiration often comes when the mind is relaxed and open. Straining too hard either in or out of meditation doesn't help. Keep it light by remembering that Spirit is ultimately in charge. Allow inspiration to emerge when the time is right. Avoid forcing Spirit along. The same could be said for worrying too much about how well you are aligning with Spirit. It is the intention more than the constant effort that is important in the process.

Ego Fatigue: When you really want something or are excited about using the law of attraction to get what you want, ambition tends to get amplified. Ego fatigue happens when you want something too much, get overeager, or try too hard. Remember that the ego always wants to play the See Me game, including "see how successful I am at using this law of attraction process." To prevent your ego from eating some serious humble pie, give your ambition a rest. Let faith and optimism have their place in the attraction process as well.

Mental Fatigue: Especially when you are in the Order Your Thoughts stage, you can burn out from too much mental strain. Creativity is often stopped when you work your mental muscles too long. The best creative efforts happen in an effortless way. Ideas and inspirations just flow onto the page, the canvas, the computer screen, or out of your mouth. If that flow is getting blocked, take a break. Distract your mind by focusing on something else or back off from the process of thinking altogether. Later, come back refreshed and with an open and receptive mind, ready for Spirit to guide it once more.

Emotional Fatigue: This takes place when you don't allow enough time for spontaneous play, lighthearted laughter, and overall joy. By taking time to play and do things just for the heck of it, without any expectation of trying to attract or get anything out of it, you help recharge yourself emotionally and ward off fatigue. Learning to reframe negative experiences through soul stories and release heavy emotional states by staying in touch with what you need also helps bring emotional energy back into your life.

Physical Fatigue: Tired of Being Tired by Jesse Hanley and Nancy Deville shares five stages of progressive adrenaline burnout. The adrenal glands give you an energetic boost, but when you are too involved in adrenaline-rush activities (always busy and living on the edge) or consuming adrenaline foods (like caffeine), eventually you wear out your natural adrenaline system. The result? Burnout. So even though it can be a rush to use the law of attraction to get what you want, it can also be a drain if you push too hard. Your body needs cycles of rest, rejuvenation, and repair. Be sure to honor this.

SPIRIT SPARK
Flow

In *Flow: The Psychology of Optimal Experience,* author Mihaly Csikszentmihalyi reveals how it is possible to be so absorbed in a creative effort that time seems to stand still, emotional problems seem to disappear, and a feeling of transcendence occurs. Flow is achieved by mastering inner subjective states that help you create something similar to the soul stories described in this book. Flow also happens when you set realistic goals for yourself and your skills match the opportunities presented to you. As related to the law of attraction, flow helps you stay in the realm of "effortless effort," which is similar to being in a state of joy and play. By enjoying the attraction process and having fun with it, you actually move the process along. And you end up having a much better time using the law of attraction, not to mention a much better time in life overall.

Part II

Living What Spirit Wants:
Practical Applications

Now that you are versed in the ten-step process for using the law of attraction in a spiritual way, I want to share with you some specific areas where you can apply these principles. The ten-step process can be applied to any area of your life. The more you learn to use it, the more automatic and simpler the process will become.

Though there are many areas I could select from to apply the law of attraction steps, I have chosen four: money, relationships, health, and the world. One of the reasons I picked these topics is because these same areas were represented in *The Secret*. I experienced both agreement and disagreement with what that book shared, which I'll discuss in the following chapters.

Chapter 14

⊘∰~

Spirit and You

Spirit and Your Money

Money! The last great taboo! It is almost comedic and ironic that people these days are far more willing to talk openly about their sex lives (on the Internet and television even), but are reticent to reveal in the slightest the true status of their bank accounts, how they make their living, and how they spend their funds. But understanding your relationship to money is important as you attract it into your life.

Wealth and Spirituality

What if you had a $5 million, $25 million, $1 billion net worth, or were able to attract it to you? Would you be able to handle that much money and live as Spirit would wish? Or would your ego kick in, making you greedy, insensitive, and unaware of how buying things mainly for your own satisfaction may be to the ultimate detriment of those around you—and even your long-term happiness? Is it possible to have a lot of spiritual and material wealth at the same time? That is what I wanted to know, and why I set out to learn how most wealthy people handle the money they possess—if they are truly earning and spending it in a spiritual way.

The good news is that most wealthy people might be considered fairly spiritual. As the book *The Millionaire Next Door: The Surprising Secrets of America's Wealth* by Thomas J. Stanley, PhD, and William D. Danko, PhD, reveals, many wealthy people tend to live more of a middle-class lifestyle and rarely flaunt the fact that they have money. Their lives are mostly stable and predictable, and they rarely live in the glamorized manner that television shows and movies present to the world. Though they come from many different spiritual traditions, they tend to adhere to a set of standard moral codes. They are also heavily oriented toward family and tend to be married to their original spouses. And their main motivation for making money was not to buy fancy cars and homes, but to have enough savings in the bank to create a sense of security, to take responsible care of their children, to retire well, and to have the flexibility to spend quality time with those they love. What this data reveals is that if you want to use the law of attraction to amass wealth in the way Spirit intends, then consider:

Before you use the law of attraction
to manifest money, it helps
to have your other priorities straight.

Priorities can also include a devotion to spiritual values (whether following a traditional religious practice or not), finding and committing to the right partner, adhering to family values, excelling at the work you are called to do, and making a contribution to your community.

THE SPIRITUAL USE OF MONEY

Whom Does It Serve? Most people no longer remember Danny Thomas, though they might still know of his daughter Marlo. At one time both were on television, and each of their shows gave a lot of joy to countless people. Though I don't know the exact details, I have heard that the general story of how Danny Thomas acquired his money goes something like this. Sometime before Danny became successful, he was pretty down and out, even struggling to care for his family. Because he was a devout Catholic, he made a prayer to St. Jude, the patron saint of hopeless causes. As part of his prayer Danny promised that if St. Jude helped him through this difficult time, one day he would repay the favor. Shortly thereafter, Danny's life turned around for the better. True to his promise, Danny used his fortune and fame to pay back St. Jude by establishing St. Jude's Hospital, which has since been responsible for helping millions of children and others who are struggling with seemingly hopeless diseases experience miracles of hope, love, and healing.

How Are You Serving It? Part of having a good relationship with money comes from also knowing that you are trustworthy with the money you have. After all, if you were deciding to give a substantial amount of money to someone, would you simply give it to an individual who would squander and abuse the gift? Or let someone have it who would really use it well? For inspiration, read *The House That Love Built: The Story of Millard and Linda Fuller* by Bettie Youngs, as an example of how to use money in a spiritual way.

Tips to Use Money Well. Make an effort to manage your finances better. Learn how to be good with your money through savings and wise investments. If need be, clean up your credit. Don't be afraid to ask for help along these lines. Set the intent to treat any money you attract to yourself with respect. Rid yourself of any notion that you are not up to the challenge that wealth might provide you with. Decide to handle money in such a way that you will be ready to take on that challenge if that is what Spirit intends for you. Attract to yourself a "money team" (bankers, financial consultants, stockbrokers, lenders, bookkeepers, accountants, tax advisors) that you can trust and who handle money in a spiritual, practical, and ethical way.

How the Ego Manages Money

If you don't have these priorities straight, you may very well use the law of attraction to visualize, affirm, and "feel" your way into amassing wealth and then find yourself only serving your ego. Examples of using money in an egotistical way include indulging in lifestyles of hedonism and greed or making monetary contributions designed only to bolster your ego's social, political, and even historical status. Even tithing 10 percent to a church, synagogue, or mosque is meaningless if you are then serving only yourself with the remaining 90 percent. And if you only use your money to help your children become an extension of your own desires for achieving recognition, fame, and further wealth, what is that really about? You see, the ego is invested in getting money for the sake of attracting attention to itself. Keeping up appearances is important to the ego. It doesn't care about soul values. It only cares about consumption and impressing others with what it has.

Perhaps this is why those who acquire money for the sake of their egos are far more likely to watch their money slip away one day. Yes, they may lose their money as *The Secret* suggests because of "fearful thoughts" that incline them to indulge in reckless spending, high living, and a tendency to run away from the responsibility of their money. They may even mismanage their wealth. But, more commonly it isn't fear, but the ego, that causes their wealth to be sucked away. At some point, others just get exhausted with the narcissistic tendencies of such a person. This results in broken marriages, rebellious and malcontent children, endless professional bills to handle personal problems (legal, medical, psychological), and even overindulgence in expensive habits like drugs and alcohol to hide the spiritual bankruptcy and mental/emotional pain within.

Is It a Money or a Vision Problem?

Since the temptations to use money from the level of the ego can often be so substantial, many people, especially spiritual people, may shy away from having money at all. In my first marriage in my mid-twenties, I attracted to myself a lifestyle that my father spoke of as consisting already of more money than he might have in his entire lifetime. My insecurities and lack of understanding about money caused me to run from that lifestyle and head into my definition of a more spiritual one that consisted all too often of being flat broke! Only during my months of meditating and journaling on wealth and spirituality did I come to understand that an avoidance of money and even great wealth is not necessarily spiritual at all!

That's why, over time, I began to say to myself, *People don't have a money problem; they have a vision problem. They don't have a clear understanding of the vision they are meant to be a custodian of if they amass money or even great wealth.* This leads me back to Perceval and the story of the Holy Grail. When you come to the altar to ask Spirit for the Grail that will restore you, be prepared to answer the following questions: "What is the Grail? Whom does it serve?"

What is the Grail? It is the symbol Jesus used at the Last Supper to remind his disciples that we all drink from one cup and that we are all here in our consciousness to learn how to love one another and participate in the one life of Spirit together. Whom does it serve? Unlike the genie in the bottle that is forced to grant the wish of anyone who commands it, the Grail can only serve the greater good. It will not grant your every wish, and it will not allow you to drink from it unless your motives are pure. Thus, before receiving the Grail, you need to examine your motives and see if you desire to serve only yourself—or your loved ones, the community, and the world.

When you imagine owning great sums of wealth,
imagine who will benefit from
your stewardship of it and for how long.

So, don't just sit down and ask Spirit to give you a million dollars, or five, or ten, a billion, or more. And don't waste your time visualizing how great it would feel to sit in your beach house or your new automobile. Spend your energy first imagining what kind of legacy you would leave behind on this planet if you really had the ability to do so. Remember, you don't have to be poor. Money can help you be the good custodian of a vision. So, get busy attracting to yourself the knowledge you need as to how you would use that money in service. Spend time educating yourself as to how you would manage the money well and how you might move beyond ego temptation to live in excess beyond what Spirit intends for you once you have it. Next to sex, money probably has the greatest power to activate the shadow within you. Money also activates the shadow in others. It is a sad fact, but once you have a substantial amount of money, other people may suddenly appear in your life who act like wolves in sheep's clothing. Even if they have good intentions to begin with, they may only take from, destroy, or manipulate you with the money you have attracted to yourself.

This is why it is so important, before you even activate the law of attraction to bring you wealth, to think of how you can build a good foundation for wealth by having the right set of spiritual values to guide you. It is also important to attract to yourself a loving, wise, trustworthy, and qualified team of people who are in alignment with the vision you have for your money and who are capable of helping you manage it well. Whether you are financially responsible for an ocean, a lake, a pond, or a puddle of wealth, you need to learn how to keep the water you are responsible for clean and pure. And you need to ensure that whatever lives within that water lives well so it can serve a higher purpose, prosper, and be loved.

SPIRIT SPARK
Talent Tale

In the Christian religion, Jesus tells the story of how God gives five talents (coins) to one person, two talents to a second person, and one talent to a third. The man with five talents invests wisely and returns with five talents more. For this reason he is blessed by God. The man with two talents likewise doubles his profits and is blessed. The man with one talent, fearing he might lose his money, buries it in the ground and returns to God with only one talent. Greatly upset with the man, God takes his one talent and gives it to the man with ten talents! What's the moral? Whatever talent (money or otherwise) God has blessed you with, it is your responsibility to move beyond your fear and make the most of that talent so that others can benefit from it. In using your talents well, you will benefit in return.

Spirit and Your Health

There are many spiritual teachers who have inspired me in my life, many of whom I have never even met. They are celebrated legends in the eyes of their fellow human beings. But one spiritual teacher who had a keen impact on me was a man named Michael. He was a simple man who worked in the bookstore and possessed incredible wisdom, a sharp wit, and a sidesplitting sense of humor! He was also, in the eyes of many, a cripple. In the years I knew him the disease he suffered from did increasing damage to his legs and arms. He would carry books from one place to another with hands that could barely hold them, and as he walked from shelf to shelf, his legs jerked and contorted in an almost comedic spasmodic fashion.

One day I was in the bookstore and overheard a conversation. I had learned about the law of attraction by then and the premise that we attract disease to ourselves because of some wrongdoing. In a callous way someone took Michael aside and asked him why he had attracted such a horrible disease into his life. In his classic witty comeback style, Michael simply looked at the man with love and a sparkle in his eyes. He declared that he had joyously attracted such a disease to teach people like this inquiring man compassion. Whether in truth Michael consciously chose his disease or not, his overall message was clear. No matter the outer appearance of the body, Spirit can shine very brightly within. And whether we are well or not, everything can be turned toward service and teach us how to love.

There is a funny thing that happens in a number of law of attraction crowds. Suddenly, people begin to get the idea that the only things that happen to you should be events that are always nice and wonderful. Especially when it comes to illness, the idea that only "good" things should happen if you know about the law of attraction can fill people with unnecessary and terrible guilt. They end up thinking that all difficult events that happen in their lives only occur because they failed to think and feel in the right way.

But we do not live in isolation from the world. Evil (as I have defined it), ignorance, and innocence are factors in what we do. Yes, negative emotions like hatred and anger, if not directed in the right way, can eventually lower the immune system and have a negative effect on the body. Yes, negative thoughts of revenge and self-loathing can make you vulnerable to accidents, cause you to indulge in eating "comfort foods," or keep you from being more aware and awake so you can make healthier choices. All true, but . . .

> *Sometimes the very stress of being of service*
> *in this world makes even the most*
> *spiritual among us subject to disease.*

How do I know this? Just look at the lives of countless great sages and saints. These people are revered by other human beings for their practically spotless devotion to spiritual values and their capacity to be near-perfect embodiments of Spirit in their lives. Yet many of these sages and saints end up suffering and even dying from various forms of disease. Why, then, do the best among us often end up with illnesses like the rest? If illness is supposed to be a result of some sort of negative thought or feeling or a low vibration, how do we account for them? *The Secret* suggests, "You cannot catch anything unless you think you can." Does this mean that the most spiritual among us who fall ill fail to know any better? Do they simply forget to think, *Oh, yes, I don't want heart illness, or cancer, or tuberculosis?* Or is there a better explanation than this simplistic notion from *The Secret?*

SPIRIT SPARK
The Meaning of Illness

Can learning to give a positive meaning to what happens to you in life actually help you live longer? Larry Dossey, MD, author of the book *Healing beyond the Body*, affirms that it can. He reveals studies that show how people who have a negative perception of their jobs are more inclined to heart attacks. And he shares how those who stay in prolonged mourning after the death of a spouse have debilitated immune systems. On the flip side many cancer patients who were in group therapy where they looked at meaning in their lives doubled their survival rates. And those who made positive meaning out of their relationships were less inclined to heart disease.

Dossey's idea of meaning is similar to my notion of creating a soul story. But he also confirms that attributing all illness to mental factors (our thoughts and beliefs) can be problematic if it produces unnecessary guilt or feelings of shame and failure. Ironically, this can also lead to people being unwilling to seek out proper medical care and to understanding that all disease may not be their fault.

What helped me solve this perplexing puzzle of how even saints get ill was discovering teachings written as far back as the early 1900s. They acknowledged that emotions like irritation, anger, fear, and worry cause bodily disorders. They warned how an inability to work effectively with any emotion (including manic bursts of happiness) can cause serious problems and disrupt bodily functioning. They talked about how wrong mental attitudes, such as distorted thinking, mental fanaticism, and frustrated idealism, can send the body in the wrong direction. And, they showed problems of congestion, overstimulation, and a lack of coordination when we shift from trying to live at one state of consciousness to another (much as would happen, for example, if you tried to shift too rapidly from a meat-eating to a vegetarian diet). Plus, they shared how at times service can lead to disease as well.

Remember, Spirit wants us to realize our oneness with everything around us, and there is no place where Spirit—and therefore our oneness—is not. Being one with Spirit often means being one with everything, including the psychological and physical ills that all of humanity suffer from. If I am attempting to identify with all that is, I can't say that I will only accept this and will always reject that. Jesus, many saints, and Mother Teresa are inspirations precisely because they embraced all of the human condition, even the unpleasant and painful states.

FOCUSING

How can you discover how your thoughts and feelings may be impacting your body? One method is focusing, a technique created by Eugene Gendlin, PhD, in the 1960s.

A psychotherapist, Gendlin and his colleagues at the University of Chicago researched the files of successful patients and found out that it was not so much what type of therapy patients received or what they talked about but how they talked about their lives that made the difference. That research led to a refined technique that Gendlin later called "focusing" (and wrote a book about by the same name). This technique has since been adapted to help discover and heal the thoughts and feelings embedded in the body. Below are the basic steps:

1. **Awareness in the Body.** Focusing is based on the idea that all thoughts, feelings, and sensations live in the body. So the first step involves closing your eyes and becoming aware of your body, especially your midsection. Then from that space get a sense of the various problems and issues you may be dealing with right now.

2. **Find the Felt Sense.** Here you become aware of what main issue most needs your attention, or awareness, and place your focus there. Also attempt to see where that issue lives within your body. This is also known as the "felt sense," which Gendlin says tends to be murky and hazy at first.

3. **Getting a Handle.** A handle is an image, sound, gesture, word, or series of words that describes your felt sense. It can include hot/cold, heavy/light, tight/loose. Or it may involve words like lost, helpless, foggy, uneasy, tense.

4. **Fit Together the Handle and Felt Sense.** Here you match up the descriptors from the handle with what you experience in your body until the two seem to fit and feel right.

5. **Asking.** Now you take time to ask, or inquire, into the felt sense to discover why it is the way it is and what it needs.

6. **Receiving.** At this stage you may receive mental insights or experience a positive shift in your body and emotions. You can receive as much as you like, or simply stop and come back to the process later if you want to go further. (For a more detailed understanding of this process consider buying Gendlin's book, *Focusing*, or check out *The Power of Focusing*, by Anne Weiser Cornell, PhD.)

Being at Ease with Dis-ease

By embracing the entire human condition, many spiritual people have even risked illness and death in the process. Despite what *The Secret* asserts, I do not believe that if a person succumbs to illness it remains in their body because it is "held there by thought." Sometimes your priorities of service are of such importance that you don't give an illness much thought at all! Illness happens; so does death. As spiritual beings, there is no reason to fear illness and death, especially if they are only a by-product of simply serving no matter what in this world. Whether you are Mother Teresa with a heart condition or a mother with cancer who gets up and loves and serves her children no matter what, sometimes bearing an illness in the body is of little importance or consequence compared to what else you are called to do. That's why . . .

> *You can still be at "ease" even when*
> *plagued by "dis-ease" if you are aligned with Spirit*
> *and being of service in this world.*

On a final note, I am not endorsing illness or suggesting we must encounter it in our lives. I am a champion of the Spirit/mind/body profession and the continued exploration into discovering how illnesses can be caused and eradicated on subtler levels by better monitoring our thoughts and feelings. Miracles can happen as people learn to eradicate their negative beliefs, change their thinking, or overcome their chaotic emotional states. Law of attraction tools like visualization, affirmation, and subtle energy body healing can produce amazing results, but the causes of disease are complex. If they were simple, we would have eliminated all disease by now. Even though we are Spirit, in our human form we are limited in our understanding. There is much we can discover and learn.

There are also numerous ways, despite having a disease, that we can still be infused with the soul and serve. Maybe we have a disease (as actor Michael J. Fox does) that ultimately serves by increasing awareness of that disease so it can better be eliminated in others. Or we serve by attempting to understand the spiritual lessons an illness has for us. And we may serve by demonstrating to others how to work with an illness with dignity and grace such as the young boy Mattie Stepanek modeled so well. We should embrace any illness with compassion, and not judgment, knowing that we are all in this together. Then, as one people, we can mutually attempt to heal disease by bringing in more love, light, and spiritual power into our world.

SPIRIT STORY
Faith and a Miracle

At only thirty-two years old, it seemed like Patti's entire life was ahead of her—until the day she got the news that she had a cancerous tumor the size of a grapefruit in her body. Patti and her husband went into despair; Patti was only given six months to live. Then they changed their focus and decided to do everything possible to learn about the cancer and see what they could do to help Patti heal.

Their solution included a radical change in Patti's diet, which included monitoring her pH balance and making sure she only ate foods that helped maintain that balance. They also engaged in daily visualizations and affirmations. The end result? Patti is thirty-five today, and the cancer remains in remission. "I can't guarantee everyone will have the results I did," Patti says, "but I tell people to never give up hope. Do everything you can. At the very least, you will feel like you are doing your part. I'm a firm believer in the saying, 'God helps those who help themselves.' I just made sure I helped God along the way, and I trusted Him to give me the results He felt best."

SPIRIT AND YOU
Key Insights

1. Before you use the law of attraction to manifest money, it helps to have your other priorities straight.

2. When you imagine owning great sums of wealth, imagine who will benefit from your stewardship of it and for how long.

3. Sometimes the very stress of being of service in this world makes even the most spiritual among us subject to disease.

4. You can still be at "ease" even when plagued by "dis-ease" if you are aligned with Spirit and being of service in this world.

Chapter 15

⁓

Spirit and Others

SPIRIT AND RELATIONSHIPS

When it comes to the law of attraction, next to money, relationships have to be the hottest topic. In my life, this is certainly the area in which I have used the law of attraction the most. A number of times I have made up my "wish list" of all of the characteristics I wanted to have in a partner. I created a vision board that included visuals of all the qualities I thought I wanted. I have attracted partners who were good looking, had a lot of money, were spiritual people, and more. But I have also failed to see the shadow in myself and others and prevented myself from attracting relationships that were really suited for me. Instead of beating myself up for these mistakes, I have learned something that many law of attraction teachers frequently neglect:

Sometimes if you attract a relationship
that seems wrong, Spirit can teach you
how something of great value
can still come out of it.

Many of my relationships that have not gone according to plan have taught me spiritual lessons. Instead of asking what relationships could bring me, I have learned the value of asking what I bring to my relationships. Instead of always expecting the thrill of fireworks, I have discovered the importance of building and maintaining a fire. When times are hard in relationships and it seems there is little to celebrate, I find quiet joy in appreciating the little things. I also value cultivating the friendship with a partner, and with one husband I was lucky enough to become a mother. As I continue to learn about the negative and unconscious behaviors I at times bring to my relationships, I learn more about how to become a more conscious and soulful human being. In short, my relationships have finally taught me they are a lot more about loving than being loved.

As you probably already know, though relationships can provide a lot of pleasure and reward, they can also deliver their share of hurt, pain, and misunderstanding. Whether intentionally or not, others may let you down. Learning how to cope with the misunderstandings and disappointments is essential to your mental health. Along with empathy and compassion, forgiveness is one of the best methods for this. In *Forgive for Good,* Dr. Fred Luskin states how loving someone doesn't mean you give them power to mistreat or abuse you. And forgiveness doesn't mean you give them a license to walk all over you a second time. Rather, Luskin shares how forgiveness helps you reclaim your power since you seek empathy and understanding and no longer stay hooked in the dance of pain and blame.

One forgiveness process my clients and I have found particularly powerful comes from Edith Stauffer in the book *Unconditional Love and Forgiveness.* She teaches how in any hurtful situation to identify and give voice to what you would have preferred to have happened instead. Too often we know what the other person did to wound us, but we seldom understand what it is we would have wanted, or preferred, them to say or do. Let's say, for example, someone failed to communicate something important to you. You feel disappointed and hurt. You decide to forgive. But you still don't understand what exactly you would have needed or wanted to have helped the process be different.

Looking at what you would have preferred, you might discover that you wished the person would have picked up the phone and notified you, or left you a quick note, or risked sharing how she really felt before acting it out in a hurtful way. The possibilities behind this step are endless, but the beauty of engaging in an exploration of what you would have preferred is that it helps you not only to forgive someone, but to understand what you needed and wanted in the situation. Knowing this opens up the possibility of actually sharing that preference with the other person so you can both learn more and get more conscious about what took place. This awareness helps prevent similar hurts or misunderstandings from happening again.

No matter what the relationship there will be spiritual lessons to be learned. Only by learning them will you be able to put the negative patterns behind you and move on to happier and healthier relationships. This is similar to knowing how to deal with your relationship baggage. As a former dating advisor for Match.com, I needed to read a lot of profiles, ideally to help people improve theirs. Often people would write that they had "no baggage," or that they were wanting someone with "no baggage." I couldn't help thinking to myself either these people were saints or they were looking for saints. Finally, I spotted one profile that made sense. This man understood that we all have baggage. He was just hoping the woman he met could store hers in a small suitcase!

How can you minimize the baggage you are carrying in your life? The most important step is to take time to learn from your relationships. Understand the mistakes you made. Take time to heal, forgive, and forget. Make sure your heart is really open to love, and to being loved by, another person. Then your baggage may not be so bad to handle, and others may even enjoy taking yours along as you spend time with them.

SOUL MATING

The idea of a soul mate is a wonderful notion. But how come once you find him or her, you often end up disappointed? Did you just end up with the wrong soul mate? Or is something else going on? I for one believe soul mates are first and foremost soulful people. Otherwise, you are really "ego mates," mating from your various unfulfilled needs, distortions, dysfunctions, desire for status and attention, and more. So how do you avoid ego mates and find soul mates? Here are some clues.

1. **Become a Soulful Person.** That's right. Unless you are a soulful person yourself, it is impossible to attract a soul mate. Even if you do meet someone who could be a soul mate to you, your ego dysfunctions will make it difficult for you see, or relate to, that person in a healthy way. That's why you need to become soulful by embodying the qualities listed in the Engage the Soul chapter.

2. **Understand Your Ultimate Destiny.** Once you understand why you are here and what contribution you are meant to make, it is easy to attract others to you who wish to make the same kind of contribution. If part of your ultimate destiny is to have a family, you will

attract a partner who also wants a family and wishes to raise children, as you do, in a spiritual way.

3. **Grow along the Way.** Learning to become a soulful person isn't always easy. And it's common to attract partners who have some spiritual maturing to do. That's why it's easy to make mistakes and attract plenty of "ego mates" as you go. Just learn from these relationships and become more soulful. This will help you increase your odds of finding truly soulful people.

4. **Learn to Be Alone.** Just in case you haven't noticed, soulful people are a rare breed. This means you may be spending time in your life without that special someone. Learning to be alone without feeling lonely is important for your spiritual development. It gives you a chance to mate with the soul within you, which is the best soul mate of all.

5. **Build Your Circle of Support.** Not all soul mates are meant to be an intimate partner. A parent, child, co-worker, friend, or boss can be a soul mate too. Once you get over the idea of having only one special soul mate, a whole new world opens up to you of rewarding, loving, and fulfilling relationships of all sorts.

BUILDING A SUPPORT SYSTEM

Over the years I have come to understand that to truly grow spiritually it is important to cultivate relationships at all levels. To begin with, though you may become intimate and close to some people in your life, ultimately Spirit will be the only intimate who will never leave you. The word *Spirit* comes from the word *inspiration,* which is related to taking breath into the body. Just as the breath is intimately connected each day to everything you do, Spirit is always intimately connected to you. It is your closest and dearest companion. That's why . . .

> ### *When you seek to attract*
> ### *any relationship, make sure*
> ### *your relationship with Spirit is secure first.*

After you put Spirit at the center of your life, it helps to build a strong support system. Though I know most people long for that one special person in their lives and often use the law of attraction to attempt to manifest that individual, I have learned that no relationship or person can withstand the strain of trying to be everything to you. I have also discovered that people who are healthy typically have very strong support groups. They have friends, family members, coworkers, and others in the community they can rely upon for support. Having this kind of network is like being a tree with strong roots. I once discovered a coaching program that asks you to generate one hundred people to be on your support list. Some of these people will be in your inner circle and know a lot about you. Others will be on the outer circle and may only be called upon to care for your home, car, health, and other things in your life that need attention. An example of how to build this circle of support follows:

Everyday People. On the outermost layer of the Circle of Support are the everyday people of your life whom you rarely know well, if at all. They help you maintain your car, keep the grocery store in good order, bring food to the table in the restaurant, and make sure the community you live in thrives. Most people are not consciously aware of how much these individuals contribute to their lives.

Especially if you are in a lonely and depressed mood, it is easy to neglect the fact that despite what you believe, you are being supported somehow and at some level. Becoming aware of this circle helps you get out of your ego and the feeling of being all alone and cut off in the world. It also helps you build a sense of appreciation and gratitude for what others are doing for you in life, even those you don't know.

Casual Acquaintances. The next layer of your Circle of Support is often cultivated out of the Everyday People layer. These are the individuals you begin to see on a more regular basis, and you may even learn their names. They might be the same person at the checkout stand, the same waitress in the restaurant, the same gas-station attendant, or the person who regularly cuts your hair. Perhaps they are a principal or a teacher at your child's school. The person may also be a librarian, church practitioner, police officer, fireman, auto mechanic, and so forth. Out of this group, you begin to refine your sense of whom you can rely on consistently to keep your life in order. Some of these people may even become so consistent in your life that they move to the next layer of your circle and become casual friends.

Casual Friends. With these people, you share the general ins and outs of your everyday life. They have a sense of who you are and you have a sense of who they are as well. They can help you build a more solid network of people who have a value system similar to your own. Though some of them may come from your everyday interaction (as was mentioned in the preceding paragraph), they more frequently come about as you attend work, events, clubs, classes, programs, and various networking groups. Frequently, you have some common interests with these people that connect you to them on a regular basis. This regular contact helps them get to know you, which means they will also be more available and understanding of your personality and various needs.

Intimate Friends. From this group of casual friends, your more intimate friends are typically found. And family members are frequently found at this level (although I understand that some people have family members who will not be close enough to reach the inner circle). Like close friends, your family members tend to know a lot about you. Whoever is in this circle, you tend to trust them with confidences about your innermost thoughts and feelings. Because they know and care about you, they tend to be there for you when crises emerge, and they can offer support, empathy, and understanding at an emotional level in ways others cannot.

Closest Intimates. As for the innermost circle, these are the people who are the closest to you. Typically, only a small number of people are found here, three to five at most. These individuals are likely to be long-term friends, family members, or intimate partners. They have a strong commitment to your well-being and offer you the deepest level of connection and satisfaction.

I have mentioned these five rings of the Circle of Support as important for you to cultivate primarily because too many people desire to find only one special person. This is understandable. But if you don't have three to five close and intimate people in your life, it can be very lonely. And if you are trying to find a lifelong partner without a network of at least casual and somewhat intimate friends to draw from, it can make it harder to attract the right partner to you. Yes, magical encounters can happen in grocery stores, bookstores, or while walking on a beach somewhere. But it helps to up your odds and live a more rewarding life (before and after you find that intimate partner) if you are busy attracting to yourself rewarding relationships of all kinds and on all levels of the circle.

SPIRIT SPARK
Too Shy to Give Intimacy a Try?

Try these affirmations to help you build your innermost circles of support:

1. Each and every day, I am open and receptive to meeting new people whom I enjoy knowing and who enjoy knowing me.

2. More and more, I have healing, loving, happy, and intimate relationships in my life.

3. I love knowing that my discernment for recognizing kindred souls is being enhanced, allowing me to find and cultivate loving and caring relationships.

4. Here and now, I heal any wounds or difficulties that prevent me from attracting and maintaining nurturing and loving relationships.

SPIRIT AND THE WORLD

As I have indicated before, there is a strange kind of deception that many who embrace law of attraction teachings call down upon themselves—the notion that somehow they should use this wonderful law to live in a protected, always happy, and insulated world. True, some books that talk about the law of attraction counter this, and I am countering this notion here as well. So does the book *Luminous Emptiness* by Francesca Fremantle, which is the best book I know of expounding upon the Tibetan Book of the Dead.

Tibetans have the idea that when we die we enter the "bardo" where we prepare to reincarnate into another life. As the soul looks down and attempts to decide what family to enter into next, the evolutionary state of the soul will incline it in certain directions and decisions, hopefully finding a family that will increase the child's spiritual growth.

Pseudo-Enlightenment

Naturally, this would make a family that is both spiritually and materially prosperous a very attractive choice. What better deal? And it very well could be if the family is truly spiritual. But there is a form of spirituality, that money especially can buy, that is not particularly helpful! This is the "feel good" spirituality that only a really wealthy lifestyle can bring you. In truth this way of living can end up being more about "self-improvement" than becoming a really loving person and getting conscious about what is going on in the world. And, it may end up using money to help insulate you so you can live in a supposedly spiritual world that is really nothing of the kind.

What goes on in this spiritual kingdom? A lot that on the surface sounds healthy and good. It may involve acquiring the perfect yoga-like body and frequently attending spas and meditation retreats. It may mean you are traveling to sacred places and sheltering yourself in exotic locations where you spend your time acquiring special spiritual teachings that the "unevolved," in your mind, haven't earned access to. This kind of privileged spirituality may also incline you to brag about having access to various spiritual teachers because your money, fame, and prestige help you align yourself with certain sects that frequently claim spiritual "status" over others around them.

The danger with all of the above comes about if at the same time you are putting your head in the sand about what the majority of people on this Earth go through, and sheltering yourself from the painful realities many people have to experience and face on a daily basis. You may even be judging others who are struggling as not having been spiritual enough to earn the special benefits you enjoy. Though there is nothing wrong with a perfect yogic body, meditation retreats, spas, sacred places, and having access to spiritual teachers or teachings, it all becomes a problem when that is all you do! This is precisely why the Tibetan Book of the Dead asserts that being born into this kind of insulated world can make true enlightenment very difficult! It can create a curious kind of deception, that you have somehow made it spiritually, when in truth you may have a long way to go. It can prevent you from seeing and making some important changes that you may *really* need to be working on.

SAVING OUR EARTH

Global warming, genocide, the human sex and slavery trade, our worldwide addiction to oil, wars of all sorts, the abuse and exploitation of people for cheap labor, the mass proliferation of assault rifles and weapons of mass destruction, the rampant rise of a lack of civility in society, the use of sexual energy in an increasingly pornographic instead of sacred way, the sexual and physical abuse of children, the killing of living people to sell their body parts for organ transplants, the proliferation of horror as an everyday staple that even small children now too often watch—all of this has been attracted to our planet through the gross misuse of the law of attraction in service to the ego. And, it is time for all of these ego creations to finally be transformed.

Friend to the World. One way these stories can change is by making a commitment to be a friend to the world. I was extremely blessed to have an opportunity to interview a hero of mine on my radio program before he passed away, Brother Wayne Teasdale. A lay monk, Teasdale not only served on the Parliament of the World's Religions, he was a member of the Monastic Interreligious Dialogue and helped draft their Universal Declaration of Nonviolence. Of his many books that have inspired me, *A Monk in the World* is one of my favorites. In this profoundly practical and spiritual book, Brother Teasdale speaks lovingly, but frankly, about our need to embrace head on many of the problems facing our world. From the problems of the poor and homeless to the call for more understanding between religious traditions, Brother Teasdale shows us all how to be a friend, not only to each other, but to the world as a whole.

How You Can Help. Each of us is responsible for attracting our unique call to service that allows us to become a greater contributor of more light, love, and spiritual power in this world. The needs of the world at this time are complex. Should you desire some practical direction on some specific ways you can become of greater service let me recommend this excellent book, *Spirit Matters,* by Rabbi Michael Lerner. Lerner gives an amazing, sweeping, wise, in-depth, yet easy-to-comprehend look at how to bring Spirit back into numerous aspects of our lives including relationships, ecology, health care, work, education, law, and more. Plus, it talks about a great concern many more people have these days, "How do spiritual people learn to maintain their hearts and souls in an increasingly spiritually deadened world?" It is well worth the read for both inspiration and application in your life.

One way to avoid the traps of this spiritual and material pseudo-enlightenment is to consider embracing two other laws, besides the law of attraction, that will also serve you. They are known in some teachings as the law of service and the law of sacrifice. The law of service is not too hard to articulate. It is simply the notion that you are here to give something back to those around you. You are not here to live in an isolated world focused only on improving yourself. A spiritual teacher I have always admired, Jack Kornfield, has illustrated this process well through the title of one of my favorite books of his, *After the Ecstasy, the Laundry!* He shares how even after the most exalted of spiritual experiences, you will still need to come back and embrace the most mundane of tasks. And not only should you embrace them, you should serve with humility as you undertake them, much as when the teacher Jesus bent down on his knees to wash the feet of his disciples. True spirituality breeds this kind of humility, as well as a desire to serve others, which is beautifully illustrated by the wonderful teacher Ram Dass in his powerful book, *How Can I Help?*

Though many find it easy to embrace the law of service, far fewer find it within themselves to embrace the law of sacrifice. In fact, in some spiritual circles they don't like the word *sacrifice* at all. Sacrifice to them implies suffering, and they want to use the law of attraction to only have the happy and easy life that comes from living out the insulated spirituality I just described. But sacrifice doesn't mean you are wanting a life of misery. A true sacrifice that is only about suffering is nothing of the kind. In fact, a long time ago I learned this definition of sacrifice—joyful giving. Mother Teresa certainly knew about this when she gave up the comfortable life of her childhood and headed into Calcutta to joyously serve the poor. And Jesus was a major example of the law of sacrifice when he was crucified on the cross.

Speaking of sacrifice, it's ironic that people often talk about finding and living their passion, but they have no idea what the word *passion* means. I certainly didn't, especially when as a teenager I actively prayed to Jesus to become a compassionate person. Later, I discovered that passion *means* suffering, and compassion implies the ability to constructively *suffer with!* So when people say they have a passion, they are really saying they are willing to make sacrifices for it, even if it means they suffer at times for something, or someone, they love. Just think of the people and causes you love. Think of the time, energy, money, resources, and "blood, sweat, and tears" you are willing to sacrifice so that others, not just yourself, can live in a better world. And, if people say they want to cultivate compassion, it means with courage, strength, intelligence, and wisdom, they want to embrace and have empathy for the suffering they are seeking to uplift around them.

In many ways, the law of sacrifice is one of the highest expressions of the law of love. What if Michelangelo had not sacrificed himself by living in contorted and uncomfortable circumstances while creating the Sistine Chapel frescoes? What if Franklin Delano Roosevelt and John F. Kennedy had not graciously dealt with their physical liabilities while serving as president of the United States? What if Martin Luther King Jr. and Gandhi had not been willing to put their lives on the line for causes they believed in? What about the countless soldiers who sacrifice their health, families, well-being, and lives to serve a country, even if it is for a cause they are not in total agreement with? What about mothers and fathers who sacrifice other opportunities so they can provide for their children? What about those involved in charitable endeavors or on rescue missions who enter countries and situations that are dangerous and disease- and war-ridden in an attempt to serve?

Whether the sacrifice is large or small, if it is done in a spiritual way, it will be done with courage, grace, and great love. And, unlike the law of attraction, the law of sacrifice is not neutral. It is a natural result of drinking from the Grail cup and in a similar way cannot be appropriated by the ego. One either makes a sincere, courageous, and dedicated sacrifice, or one does not. This leads me back to the notion of how important it is to sacrifice the desire to only live in an insulated "spiritual" world, so you can become more aware of the sufferings around you.

> *The law of service and the law of sacrifice*
> *are even more important*
> *than the law of attraction.*
> *Learn to use them well.*

SPIRIT SPARK
Changing You

Change can be a demanding process. But before you can effectively change the world, you may need to work on changing yourself. This kind of change doesn't have to be as difficult as you may think. In fact, Rhonda Britten, successful life coach on NBC's *Starting Over* television show, feels it is possible to *Change Your Life in 30 Days*—the name of one of her successful books. First this kind of change requires that you face your fears and embrace the fact that your life really can be more positive and life-affirming than it is right now. It requires a commitment to keep moving forward in a constructive way one day at a time. Along the way don't forget to acknowledge the efforts that you are making, celebrating the new you that is emerging with gratitude and love.

Think about the time we live in! Right now humanity has a massive opportunity to create new soul stories on a global level. But the old ego stories are fighting and doing their best to survive and hang on. Together we must learn to use the law of attraction with true spiritual power and in the right way. We need to unite our hearts and minds to create a global heart center that has the will, strength, and courage to drive out these old ego stories as never before.

I am reminded of an excellent book called *Night* by the Nobel Peace Prize–winning author, Elie Wiesel. It is the true account of his experience as a youth in the Nazi concentration camps, primarily at Auschwitz. Now, I had seen and read stories of the Holocaust, or Shoah, before. Though I was as deeply disturbed as always when reading about this subject matter, Wiesel's account enlightened me in ways I had not encountered before. It was the curious way people used a kind of positive thinking to avoid the impending, and even present, dark reality around them. From the ignored warnings Spirit brought to them long before the Nazis invaded their small Jewish town to the false sense of safety when they were rounded up in the ghettos to the psychic premonition and hysteria of the woman on the train to Auschwitz because she had a vision of burning bodies, Spirit's warnings were too frequently denied and discounted.

This is why en masse humanity cannot act like the people in the story *Night*. We cannot put our heads in the sand and "positive think" all of this away. We need to clearly see the reality of what is in front of us, and with the full power of the soul, use the law of repulse to drive it all away. Then we need to use the law of attraction to manifest the solutions that will help us break through into a new way of living and being. And we must continually understand how to use the law of service and the law of sacrifice to really get busy, and do something about these gross situations so we really can create a better world!

Remember to use all the laws
of Spirit to help create a planet
we can all be proud to call our home!

Facing these realities may not "feel good." But even if it doesn't "feel good," each of us needs to do what "feels right." We need to increase the power of our souls, the clarity of our minds, and the desire nature of our emotions to act for the good of not only ourselves, but the entire world! We can't afford to live insulated spiritual lives any longer. Though it is always good to undergo cycles of spiritual retreat, healing, self-improvement, and learning, it is best if they are engaged in primarily for the purpose of strengthening your ability to get out and serve! In whatever way you can, Spirit is calling you, perhaps even begging you, to approach every day with your full spiritual focus. It is asking you to bring to everything you do an increased dedication to help you become a better agent of love so you can more fully serve in the world. In both large and small ways Spirit needs you to wake up and understand that we are all in this together. Only in this way can we attract soul stories comprised of love, light, and spiritual power that will help create a world we are all proud to live in, and our children, grandchildren, and great-great-grandchildren will be proud to live in, too.

SPIRIT STORY
How Shall I Remember This Day?

It started like most days in Southern California—until that night, when the riots erupted over the now-famous Rodney King incident. Rodney was videotaped being beaten by police, and as the anger turned to outrage, it continued into violence. At first Jadine felt anxious and worried. But the next day Jadine had an inspiration. "How shall I remember this day?" she thought to herself. "When I look back on this point in time, will I only think of myself as afraid, or can I discover another way to handle this situation?" So when Jadine also heard about how the AME Church needed supplies to deliver to the riot-torn region, Jadine kicked into motion. Within one day she had approached five churches and asked for contributions to help the riot zone. She had miraculously gotten through to the AME Church to find out precisely what kind of supplies were needed. She had even gotten someone to donate a truck, and at the last minute four truck drivers had shown up, along with two couples with cell phones (they were not that common back then) to help escort Jadine and her husband in case they needed support. With this great team of people Jadine delivered a huge truckful of supplies to not only one, but three churches in the riot zone. From the entire incident, Jadine learned a valuable question to ask at any moment of crisis and concern, "How shall I remember this day?" Then kick into high gear to make sure it is a memory you will feel proud of.

SPIRIT AND OTHERS
Key Insights

1. Sometimes if you attract a relationship that seems wrong, Spirit can teach you how something of great value can still come out of it.

2. When you seek to attract any relationship, make sure your relationship with Spirit is secure first.

3. The law of service and the law of sacrifice are even more important than the law of attraction. Learn to use them well.

4. Remember to use all the laws of Spirit to help create a planet we can all be proud to call our home!

Conclusion

The Law of Attraction

Throughout this book I have attempted to reveal to you a "secret" that is much more profound and meaningful to your life than the one illustrated in *The Secret*. It is my hope this book sets you on a more solid path so you can use the law of attraction safely and well. Along these lines let me clarify succinctly the contrasts that exist between *The Secret* and *Beyond the Secret* so you will no longer be misled or confused when using the law of attraction. Here are some assertions of *The Secret* that differ from *Beyond the Secret*.

1. *The Secret:* The great secret of life is the law of attraction.

   Beyond the Secret: The great secret of life is the secret of Spirit!

2. *The Secret:* You are the most powerful magnet in the universe.

   Beyond the Secret: Who are "you"? Who is the "you" that is doing the attracting? Your spiritual self? Your ego? How can you distinguish the two?

3. *The Secret:* Ask the Universe for what you want.

   Beyond the Secret: Ask the Universe to reveal to you what it wants you to attract and manifest for the sake of service.

4. *The Secret:* It takes no time for the Universe to manifest what you want.

   Beyond the Secret: The Universe may never manifest what you want, especially if it is seeking to abort your egotistical impulses.

5. *The Secret:* Like attracts like. Thoughts are magnetic and have a frequency.

   Beyond the Secret: Yes, so strive to be and live in higher, or soul, consciousness first, or you will only attract the thoughts and magnetic frequency of the ego.

6. *The Secret:* Thoughts become things.

   Beyond the Secret: Consciousness becomes Being. Learn to be more conscious so that your thoughts are not motivated by unconscious, subconscious, ignorant, or egotistical impulses.

7. *The Secret:* Nothing can come into your experience unless you summon it through your persistent thoughts.

   Beyond the Secret: Though you are essentially Spirit, the sum total of Spirit manifests in everyone and everything. The mind of Spirit is greater than yours, and It can attract events to you that you may not have thought about or wanted in the slightest for the sake of your spiritual growth.

8. *The Secret:* You create reality.

   Beyond the Secret: Yes, "you" as Spirit create reality. But "you" as a human being with a limited consciousness and brain primarily interpret reality and can do so by creating either soul stories or ego stories. Whatever story you choose creates the direction of your dominant thought patterns and sets up the probability that you will live in either a spiritual or egotistical way on this Earth.

9. *The Secret:* A shortcut to manifesting your desires is to see what you want as absolute fact.

   Beyond the Secret: The ego is always afraid it will not get what it wants, which is why it is prone to absolutes. As you learn to be at one with Spirit, your ego is less absolute, humbler, and more willing to let things unfold instead of always attempting to direct the show.

10. *The Secret:* It is impossible to feel bad and have good thoughts.

    Beyond the Secret: It is possible to feel bad in the form of healthy guilt and shame and have bad thoughts that ultimately motivate you to want to change and become a better, more loving, and spiritual person.

11. *The Secret:* Good feelings attract good things; bad feelings attract bad things.

    Beyond the Secret: There are no good and bad feelings. Both can serve in either a positive or negative way. Bad feelings may have a constructive purpose if they are waking your ego up to the fact that it needs to develop soul values. Good feelings can have a destructive purpose if they lead you to feel good simply about indulging your ego. So move beyond if a feeling is good or bad and try to discover how to use all feelings in a more conscious and spiritual way.

12. *The Secret:* "Don't want" means you really want it.

    Beyond the Secret: "Don't want" can mean you don't want it. Both "don't want" (the law of repulse) and "do want" (the law of attraction) are valuable in this world.

13. *The Secret:* Only do what "feels good."

    Beyond the Secret: Attempt to do what "feels right." Feel good by doing good.

14. *The Secret:* Ask, believe, and receive.

    Beyond the Secret: Surrender, align, and contribute.

15. *The Secret:* What you resist you attract.

    Beyond the Secret: Yes, and the ego always resists anything that isn't for only its own good. Counter your ego's resistance by learning to surrender to what Spirit wants for you.

16. *The Secret:* To attract money, focus on wealth.

    Beyond the Secret: To attract money in a spiritual way, focus on service. Spirit will deliver what you need.

17. *The Secret:* You cannot catch any illness unless you think you can.

Beyond the Secret: Even the most spiritual people among us may suffer from disease. The causes for disease are numerous and are not always a result of your thoughts.

18. *The Secret:* Love is the greatest emotion.

    Beyond the Secret: Love is not an emotion, it is a choice. Though it may be reflected in the emotions, it exists beyond emotion in the realm of the soul.

19. *The Secret:* You cannot help the world by focusing on negative things . . . and you only add to negativity by doing so.

    Beyond the Secret: Be willing to totally embrace and see head on all the problems of the world. You are the world. Then use the law of service and the law of sacrifice to make the difference in the world you are meant to.

20. *The Secret:* We will never run out of good things because there's more than enough to go around for everyone.

    Beyond the Secret: There is enough for our needs, but not our greeds. Global warming is such a problem right now precisely because as a species we are overconsuming and pretending the good things we want to indulge our egos with will never run out. Remember, the ego is afraid of not getting what it wants. It shies away from service and sacrifice. When we are truly identified with Spirit we want less, not more, because we want everyone to have enough, not just ourselves.

And finally, I would like to summarize some lessons that I would like you to take away from this book regarding the law of attraction itself.

> *Remember the law of attraction is neutral.*
> *It can be used at the level of Spirit or the ego.*

Each of us has the responsibility to learn the secret of Spirit so we are no longer tempted to feed just our egos. Remember . . .

> *The only difference in how you use the*
> *law of attraction is whether the motive behind*
> *using it is for egotistical or spiritual ends.*

It isn't always easy to understand our true motives. The ego has a lot of tricks for deluding us. Our ignorance, innocence, and unconscious and subconscious motives can block us from a clear perception of why we want what we do. Of course, one of the safest bets is to want what is good for others, in addition to ourselves.

> *Proof that you are using the law of attraction*
> *well comes from the overall joy you feel*
> *from being filled with love, and living a*
> *good life no matter what your outer circumstances.*

Living in this way is how I know in my own life that I am residing at the center of the double dorje cross. As I often tell myself, *Regardless of my outer circumstances, if my heart is happy, my world is good.*

Again, Spirit is in everything that is and wants us ultimately to learn how to be conscious of, and loving toward, everything and everyone around us. Though I wish for everyone, as well as myself, an abundance of money, security, good health, friends, and happiness, I know that I wish far more for an abundance of wisdom, love, compassion, and the capacity to do good no matter what. That is the joy of being at one with Spirit and living as a soul and why I leave you with this final thought:

The real secret to the law of attraction is using it in accordance with Spirit. Seek to attract the wisdom regarding how to do this.

I certainly hope this book has helped you along these lines. May you be filled with love, light, and spiritual power in your search!

THE LAW OF ATTRACTION
Key Insights

1. Remember the law of attraction is neutral. It can be used at the level of Spirit or the ego.

2. The only difference in how you use the law of attraction is whether the motive behind using it is for egotistical or spiritual ends.

3. Proof that you are using the law of attraction well comes from the overall joy you feel from being filled with love, and living a good life no matter what your outer circumstances.

4. The real secret to the law of attraction is using it in accordance with Spirit. Seek to attract the wisdom regarding how to do this.